Presented to:

On this day

FIVE
MEANINGFUL
MINUTES A DAY

CHARLES R.
SWINDOLL

COUNTRYMAN

Copyright © 2003 by Charles R. Swindoll

Published by J. Countryman, a division of Thomas Nelson, Inc, Nashville, Tennessee 37214.

Compiled and edited by Terri Gibbs

All rights reserved. No portion of this publication may be reproduced, stored in a retrieval system or transmitted in any form by any means—electronic, mechanical, photocopying, recording, or any other—except for brief quotations in printed reviews, without the prior written permission of the publisher.

Unless otherwise indicated, all Scripture quotations in this book are from the The New American Standard Bible (NASB) © 1960, 1962, 1963, 1971, 1972, 1973, 1975, and 1977 by the Lockman Foundation, and are used by permission.

Other Scripture references are from the following sources:

The New International Version of the Bible (NIV) © 1984 by the International Bible Society. Used by permission of Zondervan Bible Publishers.

The Living Bible, (TLB) copyright © 1971. Used by permission of Tyndale House Publishers, Inc., Wheaton, IL 60189. All rights reserved.

The New King James Version (NKJV) ©1979, 1980, 1982, 1992, Thomas Nelson, Inc., Publisher. Used by permission.

Design: Chris Gilbert UDG|DesignWorks, Sisters, Oregon.

ISBN: 1-4041-0038-5   Printed and bound in Belgium

www.jcountryman.com
www.thomasnelson.com

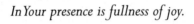

In Your presence is fullness of joy.

PSALM 16:10

JANUARY

THE GODLY TAKE
GOD SERIOUSLY.

JANUARY

-1-

Ohe of the most attractive, magnetic characteristics of Christ is His consistency. When you need Him, He is there. He's there even when you don't think you need Him! You're never too early or too late. He's never in a lousy mood nor will He ask you to call back during office hours. With Him, there's no new year or old year. He is "the same," regardless.

Jesus Christ is the same yesterday and today and forever.

HEBREWS 13:8

BIBLE READING: ROMANS 4:1; 1 TIMOTHY 4:15–16

JANUARY

-2-

There is only one YOU! Your features, your characteristics, your abilities—YOU! God designed you to be a unique, significant person unlike any other individual on the face of the earth, throughout the vast expanse of time. You were prescribed and then presented to this world exactly as God arranged it. God is personally involved in the very days and details of your life.

You saw me before I was born and scheduled each day of my life before I began to breathe. Every day was recorded in your Book!

PSALM 139:16, TLB

BIBLE READING: ROMANS 12:3–8; PHILIPPIANS 2:1–4

JANUARY

-3-

How do we live beyond the daily grind? The answer is: "A song." But not just any song! I have in mind some songs that are really old—the original Rock music, with a capital "R." They're called psalms. Those age-old compositions drip with the oil of glory that enables us to live beyond the grind. Without God's song in our soul, our long days will never end and those wearisome roads will never bend.

I will sing praise to Your name, O Most High.

PSALM 9:2

BIBLE READING: PSALM 9:1—10

JANUARY

-4-

Almost every day we encounter people who are in their own homemade boat, thinking seriously about setting forth out of the safe harbor of "life as usual." It may be a friend, a mate, a neighbor, a family member. The ocean of possibilities is enormously inviting, yet terribly threatening. Urge them on! Shout a rousing, "You're really something!" Dare to say what they need to hear the most, "Go for it!" . . . Then pray like mad.

"Put out into the deep water and . . . do not fear."

LUKE 5:4, 10

BIBLE READING: LUKE 5:1—10

JANUARY

-5-

The average American, in a lifetime, will have spent six months waiting at stoplights, eight months opening junk mail, a year and a half looking for lost stuff, and five years standing in lines of various types. Since there is no way we're going to escape all the stupid time-traps, seems to me that we're left with two choices: either we can fuss and whine about six months of stop lights, or we can take the time we've got left and spend it wisely. I mean *wisely*.

Remember what my span of life is.

PSALM 89:47

BIBLE READING: PROVERBS 4:1—13

CHARLES SWINDOLL

JANUARY

-6-

If it weren't for irritations, we'd be very patient, wouldn't we? But like taxes, they are ever with us. When it comes to irritations, I've found that it helps if I remember that I am not in charge of my day . . . God is. And while I'm sure He wants me to use my time wisely, He is more concerned with the cultivation of the qualities that make me Christlike within. One of His preferred methods of training is through adjustments to irritations.

A perfect illustration? The oyster and its pearl.

The seed whose fruit is righteousness is sown in peace.

JAMES 3:18

BIBLE READING: JAMES 3:13–18

JANUARY

-7-

There is Someone who fully knows what lurks in our hearts. And knowing, He never laughs. He never shrugs and walks away. Instead, He understands completely and stays near.

Who, indeed, knows? Our God, alone, knows. He sympathizes with our weaknesses and forgives all our transgressions. To Him there are no secret struggles or silent cries. He hears. He sees. He stays near. He who loves us most knows us best.

Search me, O God, and know my heart.

PSALM 139:23

BIBLE READING: PSALM 139:17–24

JANUARY

-8-

By accepting life's tests and temptations as friends, we become men and women of mature character. There is no shortcut, no such thing as instant endurance. The pain brought on by interruptions and disappointments, by loss and failure, by accidents and disease, is the long and arduous road to maturity. There is no other road.

The LORD sustains all who fall
and raises up all who are bowed down.

PSALM 145:14

BIBLE READING: PSALM 145:14–21

JANUARY

-9-

When we awaken in the morning, we choose the attitude that will ultimately guide our thoughts and actions through the day. I'm convinced our best attitudes emerge out of a clear understanding of our own identity, a clear sense of our divine mission, and a deep sense of God's purpose for our lives. That sort of God-honoring attitude encourages us to press on, to focus on the goal, to respond in remarkable ways to life's most extreme circumstances.

[I rejoice] to see your good discipline
and the stability of your faith in Christ.

COLOSSIANS 2:5

BIBLE READING: COLOSSIANS 2:1–7

CHARLES SWINDOLL

JANUARY
-10-

All Abraham knew was that God wanted him to move. He didn't have a clue about the final destination. No information about the neighborhood he'd live in or the problems he would have to face. He knew only that God had told him to go.

If you're waiting on God to fill in all the shading in your picture, you will never take the first step in obeying His will. You must be prepared to trust His plan, *knowing* it will be full of surprises.

The ways of man are before the eyes
of the LORD, and He watches all his paths.

PROVERBS 5:21

BIBLE READING: PROVERBS 3:6; JOHN 14:26

JANUARY

-11-

You may be one who lives your life pursuing fame and fortune, depending on the applause of others. Bad plan. To begin with, fortune has shallow rules. The winds of adversity can quickly blow it all away. Fame is as fickle as the last response from the crowd. Learn a dual lesson.

When you're praised and applauded, don't pay any attention. When you're rejected and abused, don't quit.

The reward of humility and
the fear of the LORD are riches, honor and life.

PROVERBS 22:4

BIBLE READING: MARK 10:42–45; JAMES 4:13–16

CHARLES SWINDOLL

JANUARY

-12-

Discouraged people don't need critics. They hurt enough already. They don't need more guilt or piled-on distress. They need encouragement. They need a refuge. A confidant and comrade-at-arms. Can't find one? Why not share David's shelter? The One he called My Strength, Mighty Rock, Fortress, Stronghold, and High Tower.

Be my rock of refuge, a strong fortress to save me.

PSALM 31:2, NIV

BIBLE READING: PSALM 18:1–3, 16–19

JANUARY

-13-

*L*ife is so daily. The tests that come like a flash and last no longer than a dash seldom do more than bring a brief crash. But the relentless, continual tests that won't go away—ah, these are the ones that build character.

If finding God's way in the suddenness of storms makes our faith grow broad, then trusting God's wisdom in the "dailyness" of living makes it grow deep. And strong.

That He would grant you . . .
to be strengthened . . . through His spirit.

EPHESIANS 3:16

BIBLE READING: MATTHEW 13:1–29; EPHESIANS 3:14–21

JANUARY
-14-

G od *specializes* in roots. He plans to deepen you and strengthen you. But He won't overdo it. He is sovereignly and compassionately at work. We are more impressed with the fruit. Not God — He's watching over the roots. And painful though it may be, "He who began . . . will keep right on . . . until His work . . . is finished."

God Who began the good work within you
will keep right on helping you grow . . . until His
work within you is finally finished.

PHILIPPIANS 1:6, TLB

BIBLE READING: PHILIPPIANS 1:1–11

JANUARY

-15-

With the help of a telescope or a microscope we are ushered immediately into a world of incredible, infinite design. Take your choice: planets or paramecia . . . astronomy or biology . . . or the diminutive microbes of earth—and sheer, unemotional intelligence will *force* you to mumble to yourself, "Behind all this was more than chance. This design is the result of a designer!" His name? God, the Creator.

The heavens are telling the glory of God;
they are a marvelous display of His craftsmanship.

PSALM 19:1, TLB

BIBLE READING: PSALM 33:6—22

CHARLES SWINDOLL

JANUARY
-16-

G od is in sovereign control of all of life. He is Lord of the unexpected and the unpredictable. Our times *and* our trials are in His hands.

Whether we're on Cloud Nine, enjoying His blessings, or caught in the thicket of some tangled predicament, He hasn't let us go. By His grace, He remains "for us."

He is the God of your soaring spirits as well as your perplexing predicament.

If God is for us, who is against us?

ROMANS 8:31

BIBLE READING: 3 JOHN 1:1–4

JANUARY

-17-

"I LOVE YOU." Simple, single-syllable words, yet they cannot be improved upon. Nothing even comes close. They are better than "You're great." Much better than "Happy birthday!" or "Congratulations!" or "You're special." And because we don't have any guarantee we'll have each other forever, it's a good idea to say them as often as possible.

Love is patient, love is kind.

1 CORINTHIANS 13:4

BIBLE READING: 1 CORINTHIANS 13

CHARLES SWINDOLL

JANUARY

-18-

When we pass from time into the presence of the Eternal God, we will need more than good medical assistance or the promise of a well-meaning friend. We will need a living Redeemer, whose nail-pierced hands hold our salvation.

The question is not, "Will I live forever?" Everyone lives forever. The question is, "*Where* will you live forever?"

Our Lord Jesus Christ . . . is able
to keep you from stumbling, and to make you stand
in the presence of His glory blameless.

JUDE 17, 24

BIBLE READING: MATTHEW 13:44–51

JANUARY

-19-

My marriage has taught me that I am neither all sufficient nor totally self-sufficient. I need a wife. I need her support, her insight, her discernment, her counsel, her love, her presence, and her efficiency. She is not my crutch . . . but she is my God-given companion and partner.

An anniversary says, "You don't have to make it on your own. Your partner is irreplaceable."

The heart of her husband trusts in her,
and he will have no lack of gain.

PROVERBS 31:11

BIBLE READING: HEBREWS 13:1–6

CHARLES SWINDOLL

JANUARY
-20-

God has not made us all the same. He never intended to. He planned that there be differences, unique capabilities, variations in the Body. Take the time to read 1 Corinthians 12 slowly and aloud. Those thirty-one verses tell us about His desires and designs—which are more attractive than thirty-one flavors of anything!

God has placed you in His family and given you a certain mixture that makes you unique. No mixture is insignificant.

The body is not one member but many.

1 CORINTHIANS 12:14

BIBLE READING: 1 CORINTHIANS 12

JANUARY

-21-

Y ou may be one of those individuals desperately seeking a way off the treadmill. My advice to you is to stop trying to be the top in your field. Be an excellent *whatever*. Do the very best you can with what God has given you. If His plan includes bringing you to higher levels of success, He'll do that, in His time, according to His master plan. Your part is to get out of the traffic and set your mind on kingdom priorities—stuff that *really* matters.

Whatever you do, do your work heartily,
as for the Lord rather than for men.

COLOSSIANS 3:23

BIBLE READING: 2 TIMOTHY 2:15—21

CHARLES SWINDOLL

JANUARY
-22-

Samuel Taylor Coleridge wrote, "Friendship is a sheltering tree." How true! When the searing rays of adversity's sun burn their way into our day, there's nothing quite like a sheltering tree—a true friend—to give us relief. Its massive trunk of understanding gives security as its thick leaves of love wash our face and wipe our brow. Beneath its branches have rested many a discouraged soul!

A friend loves at all times.

PROVERBS 17:17

BIBLE READING: 1 KINGS 19:19–21; PROVERBS 18:24

JANUARY

-23-

When we are lonely, we need an understanding friend. *Jesus* is the one who "sticks closer than a brother." When we are lonely, we need strength to keep putting one foot in front of the other—*Jesus* is the One "who strengthens me." When we are lonely, we need to lift our eyes off ourselves. *Jesus,* the "Author and Finisher" of the life of faith, invites us to fix our eyes on Him. He is a Specialist when the anguish is deep.

Looking unto Jesus, the author and finisher of our faith.

HEBREWS 12:2, NKJV

BIBLE READING: PSALM 25:16–22; MATTHEW 27:45–46

CHARLES SWINDOLL

JANUARY

-24-

When joy comes aboard our ship of life, it brings good things with it—like enthusiasm for life, determination to hang in there, and a strong desire to be an encouragement to others. Such qualities make our voyage bearable when we hit the open seas and encounter high waves of hardship that tend to demoralize and paralyze. There is nothing better than a joyful attitude when we face the challenges life throws at us.

How blessed are the people who know the joyful sound!

PSALM 89:15

BIBLE READING: PSALM 89:11—18

JANUARY

-25-

Married or unmarried, divorced or remarried, man or woman, young or old, whatever your situation, no matter how alluring or pleasurable or momentarily delightful temptation looks, don't linger. Claim the supernatural strength that comes from knowing Jesus Christ and, operating under the control of His power, stand strong in His might. Right now, this very moment, determine to *resist*.

Otherwise, *you will yield*. It's only a matter of time.

Keep watching and praying
that you may not enter into temptation.

MATTHEW 26:41

BIBLE READING: EPHESIANS 5:3; JAMES 4:1—2

CHARLES SWINDOLL

JANUARY

-26-

The original disciples were a handful of unlikely misfits, nothing more than a "rather ragged aggregation of souls," as Robert Coleman puts it. But the remarkable fact is that they were the same ones who later "turned the world upside down," according to the testimony of people in the first century. How can anyone explain the transformation?

There is only one intelligent answer: It was the arrival and the empowerment of the Holy Spirit. He transformed those frightened, reluctant men into strong-hearted prophets of God.

They were all filled with the Holy Spirit.

ACTS 2:4

BIBLE READING: ACTS 2:1—21

JANUARY

-27-

Some of the greatest demonstrations of courage occur in private places. At home when dealing with a child's willful defiance or in a board meeting when you're in the minority. Sometimes just staying with something over the long haul is magnificent proof of a courageous heart.

Westminster Abbey took hundreds of years to complete. Yet, because each architect stayed with the original design, the structure remained a true representation of the period of its inception. Faithfully, consistently, each architect showed quiet courage.

The LORD . . . will be with you. He will not fail you.

DEUTERONOMY 31:8

BIBLE READING: DEUTERONOMY 31:6–8; 32:1–4

CHARLES SWINDOLL

JANUARY

-28-

Worry makes you feel worthless, forgotten, and unimportant. That's why Jesus says that we are worth much more than the birds of the air who neither worry nor die of hunger because their heavenly Father feeds them. They enjoy what's there. If God is able to sustain the lesser creatures, won't He sustain the greater?

*Look at the birds of the air, that they
do not sow, nor reap . . . yet your heavenly Father feeds them.*

MATTHEW 6:26

BIBLE READING: MATTHEW 6:25–34

JANUARY

-29-

God's Word has been preserved, not merely as a collection of historical documents and geographical studies, but as a trustworthy resource—a place we turn to for assistance in living our lives in ways that honor Christ.

In the pages of Scripture, God has given us models—people, believe it or not, who are just like you and me, who, despite the odds, lived lives pleasing to Him. By faith. In obedience. With courage.

My soul keeps Your testimonies, and I love them exceedingly.

PSALM 119:167

BIBLE READING: PSALM 119:105–112

CHARLES SWINDOLL

JANUARY
-30-

Be specific in your prayer life. If you need a job, pray for a job. If you're an engineer, ask God to open up an engineering position for you, or something related for which you are qualified. . . . If you need fifteen hundred dollars for tuition, ask for that amount. Make your petitions specific.

He will surely be gracious to you at the
sound of your cry; when He hears it, He will answer you.

ISAIAH 30:19

BIBLE READING: MATTHEW 7:7–12; 18:19–20

JANUARY

-31-

W hen we repent, God promises restitution and forgiveness through the blood of Jesus Christ. He does not promise relief from any and all consequences, but He promises a relief that only the Spirit of God can give.

If we confess our sins, He is faithful and righteous to forgive us our sins and to cleanse us from all unrighteousness.

1 JOHN 1:9

BIBLE READING: 1 JOHN 1

February

THERE IS NO QUALITY MORE
GODLIKE THAN HUMILITY.

FEBRUARY

-1-

I have lived long enough to learn that God's best deliveries come through the back door. His gifts are best received when we need them most, and they always come in an understated manner, wrapped in mercy, framed with this tender inscription: "My grace is sufficient for you."

My grace is sufficient for you,
for power is perfected in weakness.

2 CORINTHIANS 12:9

BIBLE READING: ISAIAH 42:5–7; PSALM 46:1–9

FEBRUARY

-2-

Only you and the Lord know the condition of your heart. Is it soft and pliable clay, ready to be molded and shaped by the Master sculptor? You know exactly what God is asking you to do. It may be well beyond the boundaries of logic and far outside your comfort zone. You may even have a few friends telling you that what you believe He's asking you to do is wrong. Still, His leading is clear. Only one thing is needed: saying yes.

Oh, I almost forgot. You also must be willing to risk.

Teach me to do Your will, for You are my God.

PSALM 143:10

BIBLE READING: 2 CORINTHIANS 13

FEBRUARY

-3-

The Bible's timeless stories for centuries have shouted, "You can make it! Don't give up!" Its truths, secure and solid as stone, say, "I'm still here, waiting to be claimed and applied." Whether it's a prophet's warning, a patriarch's prayer, a poet's psalms or a preacher's challenging reminder, the Book of books lives on. Though ancient, it has never lost its relevance. Though old, it never fails to offer something pure, something wise, something new.

I love Your commandments
above gold, yes, above fine gold.

PSALM 119:127

BIBLE READING: PSALM 119:121–128

CHARLES SWINDOLL

FEBRUARY

-4-

Jesus met people where they were, not as they "ought to be." Angry young men, blind beggars, proud politicians, loose-living streetwalkers, ignorant fishermen, naked victims of demonism, and grieving parents were as clearly in His focus as the Twelve who sometimes hung on His every word.

His enemies misunderstood Him, but they couldn't ignore Him. They hated Him, but were never bored around Him. Jesus was the epitome of relevance. Still is.

Let all that you do be done in love.

1 CORINTHIANS 16:14

BIBLE READING: JOHN 12:44–50; 1 PETER 5:8–11

FEBRUARY

-5-

Tucked away in the folds of Hebrews 11 is a two-word biography worth a second glance, "he endured" (11:27).

Moses endured—even in his eighties. How? The same verse tells us: by focusing his attention on "Him who is unseen." He fixed his heart and soul on the One who, alone, judges righteously. He continually reminded himself that his sole purpose in life was to please God . . . to obey Him . . . to glorify Him.

By faith [Moses] . . . endured, as seeing Him who is unseen.

HEBREWS 11:27

BIBLE READING: HEBREWS 11:17—29

FEBRUARY

-6-

One woman—only one voice—saved an entire nation. Her name was Esther. As is true of every person who stands in the gap, she was willing to get personally involved, to the point of great sacrifice.

She didn't think, *Someone else should be doing this, not me* . . . nor did she ignore the need because of the risk. Sacrifice! It's the stuff people are made of who make a difference. You can make a difference. The question is, will you?

> *With one voice glorify the God*
> *and Father of our Lord Jesus Christ.*
>
> ROMANS 15:6

BIBLE READING: ROMANS 15:1—13

FEBRUARY

-7-

If it weren't for the heroic "nobodies"—faithful servants of the King—we wouldn't have any sound or lights or heat or air-conditioning in our churches next Sunday night to sing and share. We wouldn't have church staff and officers and teachers working together behind the scenes. *Nobodies . . .* exalting *Somebody.*

God has put the body together in such a way
that extra honor and care are given to those parts that
might otherwise seem less important.

1 CORINTHIANS 12: 22, 24, TLB

BIBLE READING: PSALM 147:1—6

CHARLES SWINDOLL

FEBRUARY

-8-

When we find ourselves at a loss to know what to do or how to respond, we ask for help. And God delivers more than intelligence, ideas, and good old common sense. He dips into His well of wisdom and allows us to drink from His bucket, whose refreshment provides abilities and insights that are of another world. Perhaps it might best be stated as having a small portion of "the mind of Christ."

Understanding . . . Christ Himself, in whom are hidden all the treasures of wisdom and knowledge.

COLOSSIANS 2:2–3

BIBLE READING: COLOSSIANS 2:1–15

FEBRUARY

-9-

I don't know where you are or what you face today. It's quite possible you're living under the pressure of negative criticism. Somebody may be determined to "prove" things about you that you know are absolutely false. My advice is to remain calm. Rest your case with your Lord.

Don't quit. Don't stop. Don't tell yourself that you really are the kind of person others say you are. Count on the Lord to give you the strength and the courage to stand on the truth.

The LORD also will be a stronghold
for the oppressed, a stronghold in times of trouble.

PSALM 9:9

BIBLE READING: PSALM 26:1—7

CHARLES SWINDOLL

FEBRUARY
-10-

Are you feeling crushed and confused, beaten down and misunderstood? Resist the temptation to roll up your sleeves and muster a self-imposed recovery plan. This is your opportunity! Rather than fighting back, surrender. Embrace your weakness. Tell your heavenly Father you are trusting in the strength of His power. *Look up!*

My soul waits in silence for God only;
from Him is my salvation.

PSALM 62:1

BIBLE READING: PSALM 62

FEBRUARY

-11-

Chances are good your life has grown more complicated than it was even five years ago. Over time you've collected more stuff, taken on more debt, accepted more responsibilities. Now your spiritual well is dry.

Taking time to discover what really matters is essential. . . . Don't wait for the doctor to say you've got six months to live. Long before anything that tragic becomes a reality, grow roots deep into the soil of things that really matter.

The fear of the LORD is the instruction for wisdom.

PROVERBS 15:33

BIBLE READING: 1 PETER 5:6–14

CHARLES SWINDOLL

FEBRUARY
-12-

Although deity in flesh, not once did Christ take unfair advantage of finite men and women who spent time with Him. Although Himself omniscient, He gave others room to learn, to express themselves . . . even when they were dead wrong. Never once did our Lord maneuver simply to gain the upper hand. With wisdom He held His power in check and on those few occasions when He did release it, the purpose was to glorify God.

He who believes in Him will not be disappointed.

ROMANS 9:33

BIBLE READING: ROMANS 9; LUKE 4:1-12

FEBRUARY

-13-

The answer to resentment isn't complicated, it's just painful. It requires *honesty*. You must first admit it's there. It then requires *humility*. You must confess it before the One who died for such sins. It may even be necessary for you to make it right with those you have offended out of resentful bitterness. Finally, it requires *vulnerability*— a willingness to keep that tendency submissive to God's regular reproof, and a genuinely teachable, unguarded attitude.

Christ also suffered for you,
leaving you an example . . . to follow.

1 PETER 2:21

BIBLE READING: PROVERBS 3:27–35

CHARLES SWINDOLL

FEBRUARY
-14-

The average life span may be seventy-five to eighty, but who can say you or I have that long? Since this is true, let's do our best to make the time we have count. Rather than live with reluctance, let's live with exuberance. Instead of fearing what's ahead, let's face it with enthusiasm. And because life is so short, let's do everything we can to make it sweet.

The fear of the LORD prolongs life.

PROVERBS 10:27

BIBLE READING: JAMES 4:13—17

FEBRUARY

-15-

Throughout His earthly ministry Jesus was verbally assaulted, particularly by the Pharisees. He was rejected and ignored. When that didn't stop Him, they plotted against Him. Even while Jesus was on trial, the same men who found "no fault in Him" had Him scourged and crucified. Yet at every turn, Jesus resisted the temptation to retaliate, to hold a grudge, to be defensive or resentful or bitter, to lash out in anger or revenge.

Like a sheep that is silent
before its shearers, so He did not open His mouth.

ISAIAH 53:7

BIBLE READING: HEBREWS 4:15; JOHN 10:15

FEBRUARY
-16-

Jonah and John Mark were missionaries who ran away from hardship but were so valuable later on. Peter openly denied the Lord and cursed Him, only to become God's choicest spokesman among the infant church. Paul was so hard and vicious in his early life the disciples and apostles refused to believe he'd actually become a Christian . . . but you know how greatly God used him. We could go on and on. The files of heaven are filled with stories of redeemed renegades.

In the way of righteousness is life,
and in its pathway there is no death.

PROVERBS 12:28

BIBLE READING: DANIEL 9:4–19

FEBRUARY

-17-

Nobody else is exactly like you. When you operate in your realm of capabilities, you will excel and the whole Body will benefit . . . and you will experience incredible satisfaction.

But when you compare . . . or force . . . or entertain expectations that reach beyond yours or others' God-given capabilities, then you can expect frustration, discouragement, and mediocrity.

If God made you a duck saint—you're a duck, friend. Swim like mad but don't get bent out of shape because you wobble when you run.

God has placed the members . . . in the body, just as He desired.

1 CORINTHIANS 12:18

BIBLE READING: EPHESIANS 2:11—16

FEBRUARY

-18-

When we stand strong and alone like a steer in a blizzard, looking like we can make it on our own, we easily forget that each life-sustaining beat of our hearts is a gift from God—we're really not that independent after all.

We not only need the Lord, we need each other. That need only intensifies when the winds of adversity blow hard against our souls. We cannot make it on our own.

Be harmonious, sympathetic, brotherly, kindhearted.

1 PETER 3:8

BIBLE READING: 1 PETER 3:8—12; 4:7—11

FEBRUARY

-19-

When it comes to tomorrow, our knowledge plunges to zero. You may be a Ph.D. from Yale, you may be a genius in your field with an IQ above 170, marvelously gifted and totally capable in any number of advanced, technological specialties, but you simply *do not know* what tomorrow will bring.

Thank the Lord, it is His *love* that arranges our tomorrows and whatever they bring.

Oh, what a wonderful God we have! . . . How impossible it is for us to understand His decisions and His methods!

ROMANS 11:33, TLB

BIBLE READING: PROVERBS 16:1–9; 27:1

CHARLES SWINDOLL

FEBRUARY
-20-

Without exception, people who consistently laugh do so *in spite of* seldom *because of* anything. They pursue fun rather than wait for it to knock on their door in the middle of the day. Such infectiously joyful believers have no trouble convincing people around them that Christianity is real and that Christ can transform a life. Joy is the flag that flies above the castle of their hearts, announcing that the King is in residence.

These things I have spoken
to you so that My joy may be in you.

JOHN 15:11

BIBLE READING: JOHN 15:1–11

FEBRUARY

-21-

Pain, when properly handled, can shape a life for greatness. History is replete with stories of those whose struggles and scars formed the foundations for remarkable achievements. In fact, it was because of their hardship they gained what they needed to achieve greatness.

When life becomes painful we have two choices: We can become disillusioned or we can use difficulty as a platform for placing our trust in the living God.

In faithfulness You have afflicted me.

PSALM 119:75

BIBLE READING: ROMANS 5:3–4; 1 PETER 1:7

CHARLES SWINDOLL

FEBRUARY

-22-

In 2 Corinthians chapter one, no less than three reasons are given for suffering. Admittedly, there may be dozens of other reasons, but here are three specific reasons God allows suffering:

that we might have the capacity to enter into others' sorrow and affliction;

that we might learn what it means to depend on Him;

that we might learn to give thanks in everything.

The God of all comfort, . . . comforts us in all our affliction.

2 CORINTHIANS 1:3–4

BIBLE READING: 2 CORINTHIANS 1

FEBRUARY

-23-

G od's hand on your life may be just beginning to make its mark. That steep hill you've been climbing for such a long time may be the ramp to a destiny beyond your dreams. I do not believe there is any such thing as an accidental or ill-timed birth. You may have arrived in a home that was financially strapped. You may have known brokenness, hurt, and insecurity since your earliest days—but please hear me on this: *You were not an accident.*

Your hands made me and fashioned me.

PSALM 119:73

BIBLE READING: JEREMIAH 31:3; PSALM 4

FEBRUARY

-24-

Joy is a choice. It is a matter of attitude that stems from one's confidence in God—that He is at work, that He is in full control, that He is in the midst of whatever has happened, is happening, and will happen.

Let Your priests be clothed with righteousness,
and let Your godly ones sing for joy.

PSALM 132:9

BIBLE READING: PSALM 98

FEBRUARY

-25-

God never forgets anything He promises. That's right . . . never.

God's agenda continues to unfold right on schedule, even when there is not a shred of evidence that He remembers. Even when the most extreme events transpire and "life just doesn't seem fair," God is there, carrying out His providential plan exactly as He pre-arranged it. He keeps His word.

This hope we have as an anchor
of the soul, a hope both sure and steadfast.

HEBREWS 6:19

BIBLE READING: PSALM 46:1—9

CHARLES SWINDOLL

FEBRUARY

-26-

We love the familiar. We love the comfortable. We love something we can control—something we can get our arms around. Yet the closer we walk with the Lord, the less control we have over our own lives, and the more we must abandon to Him. To give Him our wills and to align our wills to His requires the abandonment of what we prefer, what we want, or what we would choose.

Let all who take refuge in You
be glad, let them ever sing for joy.

PSALM 5:11

BIBLE READING: ROMANS 8:18—25

FEBRUARY

-27-

Back in World War II a scribble of comic graffiti began appearing on walls everywhere, proclaiming, "Kilroy was here!" It was found on walls in Germany, on buildings in Tokyo, on boulders in America. Kilroy was *everywhere,* it seemed.

God is not like Kilroy. He does not write His name on the walls and rocks of life, but He is *there*—every day, every hour, every tick of the clock! Never doubt the presence of God.

Trust in the LORD forever, for in
GOD the LORD, we have an everlasting Rock.

ISAIAH 26:4

BIBLE READING: ISAIAH 26:1–6; EXODUS 33:12–15

FEBRUARY

-28-

Though unbelieving men nailed Jesus on His cross, it occurred, "by the predetermined plan and foreknowledge of God." It was exactly at the time and in the place and by the means God had determined. And what looked to the eleven confused disciples as mysterious, as well as unfair and unjust (humanly speaking), God looked at it and said, "That is what I've planned. That's the mission My Son came to accomplish."

This Man, delivered over by the predetermined
plan and foreknowledge of God, you nailed to a cross.

ACTS 2:23

BIBLE READING: ACTS 2:22–28

MARCH

A STRONG FAITH LEADS

TO A GOOD ATTITUDE.

MARCH

-1-

C hristianity is trusting Christ, not self. Most people are trying to reach God, find God, and please God through their own efforts. But perfect trust is resting all of one's weight on something else, not on self. It's like resting on crutches to hold you up when you twist an ankle. You lean on them as your strength.

Trust in the LORD with all your heart, and do not lean on your own understanding. In all your ways acknowledge Him, and He will make your paths straight.

PROVERBS 3:5—6

BIBLE READING: PSALM 138; JEREMIAH 29:11

MARCH

-2-

When you follow God's will and find yourself in a situation that you cannot explain, *don't even try.* If you do, you'll use human wisdom, and you'll just mess things up. Call it like it is. It's another of His mysterious surprises. Practice using words like "I don't know." "I don't understand." "This is beyond me." "It doesn't make sense to me . . . but that's okay. God knows."

Man's steps are ordained by the LORD.

PROVERBS 20:24

BIBLE READING: PSALM 128:1; JEREMIAH 17:7; ISAIAH 3:10

MARCH

-3-

We reap precisely what we sow. If we sow a life-style that is in direct disobedience to God's revealed Word, we ultimately reap disaster.

The consequences of sin may not come immediately . . . but they will come eventually. And when they do, there will be no excuses, no rationalization, no accommodation. God doesn't compromise with consequences.

Do not be deceived, God is not mocked;
for whatever a man sows, this he will also reap.

GALATIANS 6:7

BIBLE READING: GALATIANS 6:1–10

CHARLES SWINDOLL

MARCH

-4-

"avid was greatly distressed because the people spoke of stoning him . . . "(1 Sam. 30:6). If ever a man felt like hanging it up, David must have at that moment. But he didn't.

What did he do instead? "But David strengthened himself in the LORD his God." He got alone and "gave himself a good talking to," as my mother used to say. He poured his heart before the Lord . . . got things squared away vertically, which helped clear away the fog horizontally. He did not surrender to hard times.

David strengthened himself in the LORD his God.

1 SAMUEL 30:6

BIBLE READING: 1 SAMUEL 30:1–6; PSALM 141:1–4

MARCH

-5-

You and I could name specific things we've gone through in the last several years that make no logical sense whatsoever . . . but that's okay. We can't figure them out. But let me assure you, God is at work doing His mysterious plan (mysterious to us). *So quit trying to make it humanly logical.* Trust Him.

Do you realize what a peaceful life you can live if you decide to live like this?

Let the peace of Christ rule in your hearts.

COLOSSIANS 3:15

BIBLE READING: JOHN 14:27; NUMBERS 6:24–26

MARCH

-6-

According to Ephesians 2:4, God is "rich in mercy." His is loaded with it! And aren't we glad?

The essential link between God's grace and our peace is His mercy . . . that is, God's infinite compassion actively demonstrated toward the miserable. Not just pity. Not simply sorrow or an understanding of our plight, but divine relief that results in peace deep within.

God, being rich in mercy, . . .
made us alive together with Christ.

EPHESIANS 2:4–5

BIBLE READING: EPHESIANS 2:1–10

MARCH

-7-

The overarching will of God is not about geography. (Where should I go?) It is not about occupation. (Where should I work?) It is not about exactly what car I should drive. (What color do you prefer?) The overarching will of God is not centered in the petty details of everyday life that we worry over. The will of God is primarily and ultimately concerned about our becoming like Christ.

Those whom He foreknew, He also predestined
to become conformed to the image of His Son.

ROMANS 8:29

BIBLE READING: JOHN 15:1–11

CHARLES SWINDOLL

MARCH

-8-

By dying in our place, as our sacrificial substitute, the Lamb of God was able to take away the sin of the world. Humanly, what seemed a cruel tragedy at the time must be seen, spiritually, as a triumph.

The suffering, death, and resurrection of Christ are the bedrock truth of Christianity, the foundation of the faith.

"Behold, the Lamb of God who takes away the sin of the world!"

JOHN 1:29

BIBLE READING: 2 CORINTHIANS 5:21; ISAIAH 53:4–12

MARCH

-9-

Jesus arrived on the planet with a mission more important than any soul who has drawn breath. Yet He didn't really get started until He turned thirty. What about all those "wasted" years? He left them to God.

We never read one time that He hurried anywhere. Or that He *worried* about anyone. What did He do with those who heard and walked away? He left them to God. And those nitpicking Pharisees? You got it! He left them to God, too.

*I glorified You on the earth, having accomplished
the work which You have given Me to do.*

JOHN 17:4

BIBLE READING: JOHN 17:1–12

CHARLES SWINDOLL

MARCH

-10-

At times God's plan will frighten you. Or you'll be intimidated by its demands. Other times you'll be disappointed. For instance, when God tells you no, to wait, or to sit tight, you'll want to argue. You may decide to fight. You might attempt to negotiate. You may become angry. But when your faith kicks in gear, none of those impulses will control you. Faith says, "I trust you, Lord. I don't understand everything, but I trust you completely."

God is not a God of confusion but of peace.

1 CORINTHIANS 14:33

BIBLE READING: HEBREWS 11:1–6

MARCH

-11-

Easter and hope are synonymous. That special day never arrives without its refreshing reminder that there is life beyond this one. True life. Eternal life. Glorious life. There is nothing like Easter to bring hope back to life. Jesus lives and so shall we!

"He is not here, for He has risen, just as He said."

MATTHEW 28:6

BIBLE READING: MATTHEW 28:1—20

CHARLES SWINDOLL

MARCH
-12-

Instead of Saturday being a change-of-pace day, it has become an opportunity to squeeze in a second job. And Sunday? A time for renewal and refreshment? You're smiling. Every time I officiate at a funeral, I'm reminded of the things that really matter. Stuff that seems so all-fired important yesterday loses its steam when you stand on a windswept hill surrounded by weather-beaten grave markers. At that moment, something within you cries: Simplify!

Better is a little with the fear of
the LORD than great treasure and turmoil with it.

PROVERBS 15:16

BIBLE READING: PROVERBS 15:1–17

MARCH

-13-

Jesus took upon Himself human flesh. For the first time in all of time, God lived visibly among humanity. During those thirty-three years He was pushed and shoved, mistreated and misquoted, tortured and scourged and nailed to a cross. He learned the lessons taught by suffering, which is why He "can deal gently with the ignorant and misguided, since He himself also is beset with weakness."

He can deal gently with the ignorant and
misguided, since he himself also is beset with weakness.

HEBREWS 5:2

BIBLE READING: LUKE 5:20–36

CHARLES SWINDOLL

MARCH
-14-

Becoming a Christian in no way ushers us into a life of perfection. If that actually happened, then why in the world is the Bible filled with counsel on forgiving others, accepting their failures, and focusing on their strengths?

I love what Ruth Graham once so wisely said: "It's my job to love Billy. It's God's job to make him good." Replace the name Billy with the name of your mate, your parent, your child, your boss, and especially your pastor.

With all humility . . . showing tolerance
for one another in love.

EPHESIANS 4:2

BIBLE READING: ROMANS 2:1–4; 7:14–15

MARCH

-15-

When some question how the Son of God could be truly human, let them look at the scene in Gethsemane, where the oil of His anguish was pressed out like the oil from the olives. Here, in the darkness of the garden, His humanity gushes out.

Jesus was not only undiminished deity, He was also, in every way, true humanity, subject to the identical feelings we have, whether it be joy or sorrow, fear or confidence, exhilarating ecstasy or sheer agony.

Jesus also, . . . suffered outside the gate.

HEBREWS 13:12

BIBLE READING: MATTHEW 26:36–46

CHARLES SWINDOLL

MARCH

-16-

The psalmist was correct: The heavens *do* indeed tell of the glory of God . . . their expanse *does* indeed declare the work of His hands (Ps. 19:1).

And when you mix that unfathomable fact with the incredible reality that He cares for each one of us right down to the last, tiniest detail, the psalmist is, again, correct: such knowledge is beyond me . . . I cannot even imagine it (Ps. 139:6).

The heavens are telling of the glory of God;
and their expanse is declaring the work of His hands.

PSALM 19:1

BIBLE READING: PSALMS 19:1–6; 139:1–12

MARCH

-17-

There has never been a more unfair, illegal, or shameful set of trials conducted in the history of jurisprudence than the six trials that led to the crucifixion and death of the Lord Jesus Christ. In this, however, there is a paradox: From those acts of injustice, the justice of God was satisfied. As men poured out their wrath upon Christ at His trials and His death, God's wrath against sin was completely released upon Christ at the cross.

While we were yet sinners, Christ died for us.

ROMANS 5:8

BIBLE READING: ISAIAH 50:4–7; 52:13–15

MARCH

-18-

When God plans to use us, He puts us through the paces. He allows a certain amount of suffering. God may use the strong, stubborn, independent individualists in the world, but not long-term. He much prefers the humble, the broken, the bruised, even the crushed. He works much more effectively in the lives of people who've learned they can't make it on their own, especially those who acknowledge they desperately need God and others.

He who pursues righteousness and
loyalty finds life, righteousness and honor.

PROVERBS 21:21

BIBLE READING: MARK 12:28—34

MARCH

-19-

Barabbas missed his cross because another man took his place.

Jesus hung on the cross intended for Barabbas, just as He hung on the cross in our place. Like Barabbas we were dead in our trespasses and sins until Jesus' crucified body released the blood of substitution. Like Barabbas, we were condemned to die until Jesus took our place.

Like Barabbas, we have been set free, and it is freedom for eternity.

The LORD has caused the iniquity of us all to fall on Him.

ISAIAH 53:6

BIBLE READING: JOHN 3:16—18

CHARLES SWINDOLL

MARCH
-20-

Perhaps you have just stumbled. You feel guilty, you feel like a failure. You wish like crazy you had never opened your mouth . . . or done what you did. You're miserable, discouraged, and you'd like to hide. Ridiculous! Get out of that pool of self-pity, brush off the dirt with the promise of God's forgiveness—and move on!

Stumblers who give up are a dime a dozen. Stumblers who *get up* are rare. They're priceless.

We all stumble in many ways.

JAMES 3:2

BIBLE READING: PSALM 37:23–24; HEBREWS 4:12–16

MARCH

-21-

Christ's hands and feet would be pierced. His bones would be pulled out of joint. His clothing would be divided, and they would cast lots for His garments. He would be the object of scorn and mockery. Remarkably, God gave all of those details some nine hundred and fifty years before the fact.

The death of Jesus opened the pathway to heaven—a pathway prepared and paved with His blood.

They pierced my hands and my feet. . . . They divide my garments among them, and for my clothing they cast lots.

PSALM 22:16, 18

BIBLE READING: PSALM 22

CHARLES SWINDOLL

MARCH

-22-

As I attempt to find some secret clue to Paul's joy, I have to conclude that it was his confidence with God. To Paul, God was in full control of everything. Everything! If hardship came, God permitted it. If pain dogged his steps, it was only because God allowed it. If he was under arrest, God remained the sovereign director of his life.

My point? God is no distant deity but a constant reality, a very present help whenever needs occur. So? So live like it. And laugh like it!

Rejoice in the Lord always; again I will say, rejoice!

PHILIPPIANS 4:4

BIBLE READING: PSALM 43

MARCH

-23-

J esus took a cup, offered a prayer of thanks, and said to His disciples, "Drink from it, all of you."

The same word that is used here for "cup" is used later when Jesus prays in the Garden of Gethsemane: "Father, if it be Your will, let this cup pass from me; nevertheless, not My will but Yours be done."

Out of obedience to the Father, Jesus took the cup of death, willing to pay for the sins of the world.

When He had taken a cup . . .
He gave it to them, saying, "Drink from it, all of you."

MATTHEW 26:27

BIBLE READING: MATTHEW 26:26–46

CHARLES SWINDOLL

MARCH

-24-

Job did not say, "When He has tried me, I will make a million!" Or, "When He has tried me, I'll get everything back that I lost." Or, "When He has tried me, my wife will say she's sorry and will make things right." No, it's not the externals that are promised, it's the internals. The Lord promised Job, "When the process is finished, you'll come forth as *gold*. Then, you'll be ready to serve me where I choose."

He knows the way I take; when He
has tried me, I shall come forth as gold.

JOB 23:10

BIBLE READING: JEREMIAH 32:40; PSALM 95:7;
DEUTERONOMY 31:6

MARCH
-25-

In the judicial process of interrogation, Pilate heard Christ refer to "everyone who is of the truth," to which Pilate replied, "What is truth?" Pilate never waited for an answer. He whirled away in confused disgust. He should have stopped running and waited for the answer. Jesus could have told him that He alone had satisfying words of life . . . for He alone is "the way, the truth, and the life" (John 14:6).

We are of the truth, and . . . assure our heart before Him.

1 JOHN 3:19

BIBLE READING: MATTHEW 11:25–30; PSALM 62:5–8

CHARLES SWINDOLL

MARCH

-26-

"Be on the alert, stand firm in the faith, act like men, be strong." Those words were written by a man who practiced what he penned. Paul was his name. "Guts" could have been his nickname. With single-minded determination, the rugged apostle hitched in his belt and pressed on.

Even a cursory review of his life makes most Christians of today look like pantywaists.

Be on the alert, stand firm
in the faith, act like men, be strong.

1 CORINTHIANS 16:13

BIBLE READING: 1 CORINTHIANS 16:13–24

MARCH

-27-

What a contrast we have at the cross. God's perfect sacrifice—His Lamb—hangs there in agony, giving His life, shedding His blood for the sins of the world. Heaven stands breathless, poised between life and death, as the salvation of the world is being completed. And at the feet of the Lord Jesus, four coarse, sin-hardened soldiers are shooting dice for His garments. The study is breathtaking.

The one who comes to Me I will certainly not cast out.

JOHN 6:37

BIBLE READING: JOHN 19:23—25

CHARLES SWINDOLL

MARCH
-28-

Godly people possess an attitude of willing submission to God's will and ways. Whatever He says goes. And whatever it takes to carry it out is the very thing the godly desire to do.

He who has My commandments
and keeps them is the one who loves Me.

JOHN 14:21

BIBLE READING: 1 JOHN 5:3–5; PSALM 119:30–32

MARCH

-29-

"Forgive them." What an amazing request! If someone pressed a crown of sharp thorns on your head, stripped you naked for all the world to see, brutally punched you in the face, drove nails into your hands and feet and lifted you up on a cross to die, would you pray that kind of prayer?

Today, at the slightest offense we are ready to retaliate, defend ourselves, and fight back. Yet at His greatest moment of agony, Jesus sincerely prayed, "Forgive them."

*"Father, forgive them; for they
do not know what they are doing."*

LUKE 23:34

BIBLE READING: ACTS 6:8; 7:54–60

CHARLES SWINDOLL

MARCH

-30-

The Bible is God's inspired truth. It is wholly trustworthy, for God is trustworthy. It is our sacred guide, written for our instruction. But it is not some kind of rabbit's foot we carry about, hoping for good luck. It is to be read intelligently, interpreted carefully, treated respectfully, handled wisely, and applied correctly.

Remember the word to Your servant,
in which You have made me hope.

PSALM 119:49

BIBLE READING: PSALM 119:49–56

MARCH

-31-

One of the great themes of Christianity is triumphant hope. Not just hope as in a distant, vague dream, but *triumphant* hope, the kind of hope where all things end right. In the midst of the struggles and the storms and the sufferings of life, we can advance our thoughts beyond today and see relief . . . triumph . . . victory. Because, in the end, God does indeed win.

The LORD gives grace and glory; no good thing does He withhold from those who walk uprightly.

PSALM 84:11

BIBLE READING: PSALM 84

CHARLES SWINDOLL

APRIL

BEHIND THE MAZE

IS THE MASTER.

APRIL

-1-

In His dying moments, Christ concerned Himself with the welfare of His mother. She had been very much in the background throughout His public ministry. Yet at the time of His death, Jesus challenged John to care for her.

God rewards those who care. He will honor you if you will honor your parents. You never grow too old to spend time with them, to glean from their wisdom, and to make certain they know how much you love them.

Honor your father and
your mother, that your days may be prolonged.

EXODUS 20:12

BIBLE READING: JOHN 19:25—27

CHARLES SWINDOLL

APRIL

-2-

We live in a culture that regularly confuses humanity with deity. It's the kind of sloppy theology that suggests God sits on the edge of heaven thinking, *Wonder what they'll do next?* How absurd! God is omniscient. This implies, clearly, God never learns anything, our sinful decision and evil deeds notwithstanding. Nothing ever surprises Him. From the moment we're conceived to the moment we die, we remain safely within the frame of His watchful gaze as well as His sovereign plan.

This is God, our God forever
and ever; He will be our guide even to death.

PSALM 48:14, NKJV

BIBLE READING: HEBREWS 1:5–14

APRIL

-3-

This planet was designed by God so that it would support one thing: life. Without life, earth would be another planetary wasteland. It would be like a wedding without a bride . . . a car without gears and wheels. Why life? Because only through life can matter understand God and glorify its Maker! Only through faith in the Lord Jesus Christ can the designed know and glorify the designer.

He makes the clouds His chariot;
He walks upon the wings of the wind.

PSALM 104:3

BIBLE READING: PSALM 104:1–17

APRIL

-4-

When it comes to "training up a child in the way he should go," you've got the inside lane, Mom and Dad. No teacher or coach, grandparent or sibling, counselor or minister will have the influence on your kid that you are having. So— take it easy! Remember "children are wet cement." They take the shape of your mold. They're learning even when you don't think they're watching. And those little guys and gals are plenty smart. They read looks as well as books.

Train up a child in the way he should go,
even when he is old he will not depart from it.

PROVERBS 22: 6

BIBLE READING: DEUTERONOMY 4:9, 40; PROVERBS 22:15

APRIL

-5-

God the Father forsook His Son on the cross, so that He might never have to forsake us now. That, in one sentence, is the answer to the question, "My God, My God, why have You forsaken Me?" God the Father forsook His Son once for all that He might never have to forsake His adopted sons and daughters now or evermore.

"I will never desert you, nor will I ever forsake you."

HEBREWS 13:5

BIBLE READING: MATTHEW 27:46; JOSHUA 1:5–9

APRIL

-6-

Heaven. It is a place of eternal bliss; it's the place of God's presence forever.

We hear "heavenly" music today, and we think it's going to be like that in heaven. But actually, the most beautiful music on earth sounds like *Chopsticks* when placed alongside the real heavenly music. Handel's *Hallelujah Chorus* will be nothing compared to the myriad of angels who will sing in antiphonal voice as we join them in praises to the Lamb of God.

Hallelujah! For the Lord our God, the Almighty, reigns.

REVELATION 19:6

BIBLE READING: REVELATION 5:11—14; 19:1—6

APRIL

-7-

L ots of material is available on motivation. Plenty of advice is floating around on setting goals and establishing priorities. All of it is insightful and needed, no doubt about it.

But let's hear it for the opposite end for a change. Let's extol the virtues of sticking with something until it's *done*. Of hanging tough when the excitement and fun fade into discipline and guts. Listen to the Master whisper: *let us not lose heart.*

> *Let us not lose heart in doing good, for in*
> *due time we will reap if we do not grow weary.*

GALATIANS 6:9

BIBLE READING: 1 CORINTHIANS 15:58; 1 PETER 5:8, 10

APRIL

-8-

Christ died and rose again—on our behalf. The Law said that where there was sin, there must be death.

We know that Christ's death completed the work of atonement because God raised Him from the dead. If God had not been satisfied in the death of His Son, the Son would have remained a lifeless corpse in the tomb. When the Father raised the Son, it represented His "stamp of approval" on the transaction.

He died for all, . . . and rose again on their behalf.

2 CORINTHIANS 5:15

BIBLE READING: 2 CORINTHIANS 5:1-15

APRIL

- 9 -

I find God's incomprehensibility absolutely refreshing, especially in a day when managerial moguls prance like peacocks and deified athletes strut their stuff. At a time when one-upmanship and human intimidation have become an art form, it is delightful to be reminded anew that "Our God is in the heavens" and that "He does whatever He pleases."

After all, He is the Maker of heaven and earth.

Our God is in the heavens; He does whatever He pleases.

PSALM 115:3

BIBLE READING: PSALM 114; 115:1–8

CHARLES SWINDOLL

APRIL

-10-

It occurs to me that I've never met anyone young and patient. (To be honest, I've not met many *old* and patient folks either). We're all in a hurry. We don't like to miss one panel of a revolving door. Patience comes hard in a hurry-up society. Yet, it's an essential quality, cultivated only in extended periods of waiting.

The testing of your faith produces patience.

JAMES 1:3, NKJV

BIBLE READING: JAMES 1:1—12

APRIL

-11-

Death is not the end, but the beginning. It is not termination, but promotion. And this we know, because Jesus arose from the dead! We shall indeed be risen again. The perishable shall become imperishable, and the mortal will become immortal on that great day.

The resurrection is the key to the mystery of eternity.

Christ has been raised from the dead,
the first fruits of those who are asleep.

1 CORINTHIANS 15:20

BIBLE READING: 1 CORINTHIANS 15:20—28

CHARLES SWINDOLL

APRIL

-12-

These minds of ours are like bank vaults awaiting our deposits. If we regularly deposit positive, encouraging, and uplifting thoughts, what we withdraw will be the same. And the interest paid will be joy. The secret lies in our mind-set—the things we fix our minds on.

Fix your thoughts on what is true and good and right.

PHILIPPIANS 4:8, TLB

BIBLE READING: Psalm 94:17–23

APRIL

-13-

Fragility is not a virtue extolled in Scripture. Saints with thin skin get distracted and, shortly thereafter, discouraged. There's a long, demanding course to be run, most of which takes place in the trenches and without applause. . . .

Endurance is the secret, not popularity.

I am well content with . . . difficulties, for Christ's sake.

2 CORINTHIANS 12:10

BIBLE READING: 2 CORINTHIANS 11:23–33; 12:7–10

CHARLES SWINDOLL

APRIL

-14-

This world is not out of control, spinning wildly through space. Nor are earth's inhabitants at the mercy of some blind, random fate. When God created the world and set the stars in space, He also established the course of this world and His plan for humanity.

O LORD my God, You are very great; . . .
[You] established the earth upon its foundations.

PSALM 104:1, 5

BIBLE READING: JOB 38:12–41

APRIL

-15-

We have to learn to trust God one day at a time.

Did you notice that God never told Elijah what the second step would be until he had taken the first step? God told His prophet to go to Ahab. When Elijah got to the palace, God told him what to say. After he said it, God told him, "Now, go to the brook." He didn't tell Elijah what was going to happen at the brook." Elijah didn't know the future, but he did have God's promise: "I'll provide for you there."

I will instruct you and
teach you in the way which you should go.

PSALM 32:8

BIBLE READING: 1 KINGS 17; ISAIAH 49:16

APRIL

-16-

There were seven sayings that Christ uttered from the cross, commonly called the seven last words of Christ. One of the words our Lord cried out was *Tetelestai!* Translated, it means, "It is finished!" *Telos* is the root Greek term, the same root of the word translated *perfect*. Paul was saying, "He who began a good work in you when you were converted ten years ago, Philippians, will bring it to completion. It will be finished! Jesus will see to it. And that gives me joy."

He who began a good work in you
will perfect it until the day of Christ Jesus.

PHILIPPIANS 1:6

BIBLE READING: PHILIPPIANS 1:1—11

APRIL

-17-

God's plan includes all promotions and demotions. His plan can mean both adversity and prosperity, tragedy and calamity, ecstasy and joy. His plan is at work when we cannot imagine why. It is at work through all disappointments, broken dreams, and lingering difficulties. And even when we cannot fully fathom why, He knows. Even when we cannot explain the reasons, He understands. And when we cannot see the end, He is there, nodding, "Yes, that's My plan."

From Him and through Him and to Him are all things.

ROMANS 11:35

BIBLE READING: ROMANS 11:34–36

APRIL

-18-

L ists are everywhere. The publishing world has its best-seller list, the music world its gold and platinum album lists, the financial world its Fortune 500 list.

The prophet Micah lists the absolute basics "required" by the Lord. It's not a long list. In fact it's short and simple. So the next time you feel that living for God is getting too complicated, blow the dust off Micah's list: *to do justice, to love kindness, to walk humbly with God.*

What does the LORD require of you but to do justice,
to love kindness, and to walk humbly with your God?

MICAH 6:8

BIBLE READING: PHILIPPIANS 1:6–11

APRIL

-19-

In a "Peanuts" cartoon, Lucy says to Snoopy: "There are times when you really bug me, but I must admit there are also times when I feel like giving you a big hug."

Snoopy replies, "That's the way I am . . . huggable and buggable."

And so it is with our relationships in God's family. We may not always agree, but can't we be *agreeable?*

That I may come to you . . .
and find refreshing rest in your company.

ROMANS 15:32

BIBLE READING: ROMANS 15:14–33

CHARLES SWINDOLL

APRIL
-20-

Who has ever given God counsel? No one! His mind, His judgements are unsearchable. His ways are "unfathomable." No human being can predict or plumb the depths of God's will. Try though we may, we cannot unravel the tapestry of His plan.

Yet, wonder of wonders, God can be known deeply by the hearts of those created in His image.

*Who has known the mind
of the LORD, or who became His counselor?*

ROMANS 11:34

BIBLE READING: ROMANS 11:33–36; ISAIAH 55:9

APRIL

-21-

Who would have guessed five years ago that you'd be doing what you're doing right now? Not one of us. And I have news for you. You have no idea what the next five years will bring. The future is just as uncertain and exciting and full of risk and wonder as the past five years. But whatever that future brings is also absolute, immutable, unconditional, and in complete harmony with God's nature and plans.

O LORD, lead me in your righteousness; . . .
make Your way straight before me.

PSALM 5:8

BIBLE READING: 2 TIMOTHY 1:8-14

CHARLES SWINDOLL

APRIL

-22-

We need to learn the deep and enduring value of the hidden life.

When I think of hidden lives, I think of mothers of small children. I think of compassionate men and women who are now caring for elderly parents. I think of highly capable or qualified individuals, who, it seems, for the time being, are completely useless. I think of students still in the classroom, preparing, preparing, preparing. It's the hidden life—the life where lasting lessons are learned.

God is the strength of my heart and my portion forever.

PSALM 73:26

BIBLE READING: PSALM 73:23—28

APRIL

-23-

You want to know who's in charge around here? The One who called the space into being, the One who put clouds in place, the One who established the atmosphere in which we're able to live, and One who separated the seas and the dry land, who gave you breath for your lungs and the ability to think. The One who placed you here, now, in time, for His purpose, and the One who with the snap of His divine finger will pull you from life into eternity. Mysterious though our lives may seem, God, and God alone, is in charge.

God is my stronghold, the God who shows me lovingkindness.

PSALM 59:17

BIBLE READING: PSALM 59:9–17

CHARLES SWINDOLL

APRIL

-24-

God keeps His promises. It's a major part of His immutable nature. He doesn't hold out hope with nice-sounding words, then renege on what He said He would do. God is neither fickle nor moody. And He never lies. As my own father used to say of people with integrity. "His word is His bond."

This hope we have as an anchor
of the soul, a hope both sure and steadfast.

HEBREWS 6:19

BIBLE READING: HEBREWS 6:9–20

APRIL

-25-

For three years, Paul lived somewhere in the desert—in solitude, quietness, and obscurity.

Do the math and you come up with well over one thousand days unaccounted for in his life. A thousand plus days he most likely spent alone. Thinking. Praying. Listening to the Lord.

I'm convinced it was there, in that barren place of obscurity, that Paul developed his theology. He met God, intimately and deeply.

I have suffered the loss of all things,
and count them but rubbish so that I may gain Christ.

PHILIPPIANS 3:8

BIBLE READING: PHILIPPIANS 3:1–11

APRIL

-26-

There is a mystery, an aura, about the living God that is designed to force us to trust Him, even when we cannot figure Him out (which is most of the time). Why? Because, He is inexplicable, He is unfathomable, He is infinite.

The mystery is purposeful, because His overall plan is profound. And let's not forget that His plan is not designed to make us comfortable; it is designed to make us more like Christ.

There is no partiality with God.

ROMANS 2:11

BIBLE READING: JOB 38:1—11

APRIL

-27-

In this life, we have focus choices. We can focus on ourselves, we can focus on our circumstances, we can focus on other people, or we can focus on God. When you think biblically, you focus first on God. Regardless of what you want, regardless of the circumstances you're under, regardless of what others say or think, regardless of how you feel. God and God alone is working out His great plan. And in the final tally, it will be fabulous!

The Lord will accomplish that which concerns me.

PSALM 138:8

BIBLE READING: DEUTERONOMY 8:18–20

CHARLES SWINDOLL

APRIL

-28-

God is working His will in us. He is shaping us into the image of Christ, which means His Son's discipline, His endurance, His faithfulness, His purity, His attitude, His whole philosophy of life. God's goal is to make us like His dear Son. And that is a lifetime task . . . our lifetime, that is.

Those whom I love, I reprove and discipline.

REVELATION 3:19

BIBLE READING: PROVERBS 3:11–12; 1 CORINTHIANS 11:32

APRIL

-29-

We need to give one another stretching space—room to respond and react in a variety of ways, even as our infinite Creator molded a variety of personalities. This will require a ritual burning of our list of expectations. For some of us, it could make quite a bonfire. It will also mean we stop anticipating the *ideal* and start living with the real—which is always checkered with failure and imperfection. Let's serve one another in love.

Through love serve one another.

GALATIANS 5:13

BIBLE READING: PSALM 5:3; MATTHEW 20:1–16

APRIL

-30-

Specific pain enables us to comfort others specifically. If you lose your child, God uses you in the life of a mother as she endures the loss of her child. If you've struggled through the dark tunnel of divorce, no one understands as you do when a friend tells you a spouse has just walked out the door.

I've never had cancer. I couldn't offer the depth of comfort you could if you've had that disease. That's how God works.

God . . . comforts us in all our affliction.

2 CORINTHIANS 1:3–4

BIBLE READING: 2 CORINTHIANS 1:3–11

MAY

OUR BEST WORK IS
DONE ON OUR KNEES.

MAY

- 1 -

God not only struck the spark that gave you and me life, He continues to prompt each heartbeat in every chest. And what He does for us as individuals, He does for the vast universe about us. Furthermore, what God creates, God sustains. As the Scriptures state so clearly, He upholds all things by His power. Think of it . . . *all things!*

All things have been created by Him and
. . . in Him all things hold together.

COLOSSIANS 1:16–17

BIBLE READING: COLOSSIANS 1:13–22

CHARLES SWINDOLL

MAY

-2-

In spite of his brothers' cruel mistreatment, subsequent slavery in Egypt, false accusations from Mrs. Potiphar (resulting in being dumped into a dungeon for years), Joseph steered clear of bitterness. As a matter of fact, He ultimately told his brothers, "God turned into good what you meant for evil" (Gen. 50:20, TLB). Talk about incredible perspective regarding life's arrows! Arrows don't change a person's direction. They merely deepen his or her character.

Seek the LORD and His strength; seek His face continually.

PSALM 105:4

BIBLE READING: PSALM 105:1—7

MAY

-3-

There would never have been an Isaac without a Sarah, a Moses without a Jochebed, a Samuel without Hannah, a John without an Elizabeth, a Timothy without a Eunice, or a John Mark without a Mary.

These men were the men they were, in great part, because of the mothers they had. The hidden secret of that winning combination? Mother with child—just that simple. So, please . . . moms, stay at it.

Her children rise up and bless her.

PROVERBS 31:28

BIBLE READING: PROVERBS 31:10—31; 2 TIMOTHY 1:1—5

CHARLES SWINDOLL

MAY

-4-

I said, "I will guard my ways, that I may not sin with my tongue; I will guard my mouth as with a muzzle" (Ps. 39:1). That's what it takes, friends and neighbors. A conscious, tight muzzle on the muscle in your mouth—with emphasis on *conscious.*

To accomplish that disciplined objective, I offer these three suggestions:

Think first. Talk less. Start today.

The things that proceed out of the mouth come from the heart.

MATTHEW 15:18

BIBLE READING: MATTHEW 15:10—20

MAY

-5-

In her bestseller, *What is a family?*, Edith Schaeffer devotes her longest chapter to the idea that a family is *a perpetual relay of truth*. A place where principles are honed on the anvil of everyday living. Where character traits are sculptured under the watchful eyes of moms and dads.

And how is this done? Over the long haul. This race is not a sprint, it's a marathon—practiced around the track hour after hour when nobody is looking.

Teach [these words] diligently to your sons
and talk of them when you sit in your house.

DEUTERONOMY 6:7

BIBLE READING: DEUTERONOMY 6:4–9; LUKE 2:21–51

MAY

-6-

While our entire world is sinking in the quagmire of human opinions, theories, philosophies, and dreams, our Lord invites us to stand firmly on the rock of reality. And what does the realist mind-set include? It includes such things as:

- Man is a depraved sinner, terribly in need.
- Our only hope is in Jesus Christ—His death and resurrection.
- Receiving Him brings instant forgiveness and eternal grace.

Set your mind on the things above,
not on the things that are on earth.

COLOSSIANS 3:2

BIBLE READING: JOB 19:25–27; COLOSSIANS 2:8–23

MAY

-7-

G od brings about birthdays . . . not as deadlines but *lifelines.* He builds them into our calendar once every year to enable us to make an annual appraisal, not only of our length of life but of our depth. Not simply to tell us we're growing older . . . but to help us determine if we are also growing deeper.

The psalmist gives us the perfect prayer to pray every year our birthday rolls around:

So teach us to number our days,
that we may present to You a heart of wisdom.

PSALM 90:12

BIBLE READING: PSALM 105:1—7

MAY

-8-

The difference between something good and something great is attention to detail. That is true of a delicious meal, a well-kept home, a church, our attire, a business, a lovely garden, a sermon, a teacher, a well-disciplined family.

Let's make a long-term commitment to quality control. Let's move out of the thick ranks of the mediocre and join the thin ranks of excellence. . . . I'm ready if you are.

Whatever your hand finds to do, do it with all your might.

ECCLESIASTES 9:10

BIBLE READING: PROVERBS 19:1—14

MAY

-9-

A word of encouragement is in order for all you mothers! Your role is, clearly, the single most important in society. Your place in your family's life is absolutely strategic. Those children you are rearing may not stop to tell you, but you need to know—it's worth all the effort.

Mary had her son for thirty years. And though she survived Him, she would never forget His compassionate concern and tender courage. Who knows? He probably learned both from her.

Let her rejoice who gave birth to you.

PROVERBS 23:25

BIBLE READING: LUKE 1:42, 46–55

CHARLES SWINDOLL

MAY

-10-

The shadow of suffering falls across every path. Even the One who left heaven when He came to live among us was inseparably linked to that shadow. As one of His own followers later wrote, "They who were His own . . . did not welcome Him."

We must be prepared to suffer and, in fact, to die (to self) before we can live the life our Savior has designed for us to live.

He came to that which belonged to Him . . .
and they who were His own did not receive Him and
did not welcome Him.

JOHN 1:11, TLB

BIBLE READING: ISAIAH 53:1–3; 2 CORINTHIANS 7:10

MAY

-11-

Busyness substitutes shallow frenzy for deep friendship. It promises satisfying dreams but delivers hollow nightmares. It feeds the ego but starves the inner man. It fills a calendar but fractures a family. It cultivates a program but plows under priorities.

Starting today, refuse every possible activity that isn't absolutely necessary. Sound ruthless? So is the clock. So is your health. Start saying no.

It is vain for you to rise up early, to retire late.

PSALM 127:2

BIBLE READING: ECCLESIASTES 2:22—26

CHARLES SWINDOLL

MAY

-12-

The best platform to build a case for Christianity at work rests on six massive pillars: integrity, faithfulness, punctuality, quality workmanship, a pleasant attitude, and enthusiasm.

It will help you do a super job if you'll remember that there's no sacred-secular distinction to Titus 1:15: *To the pure, all things are pure.* That means your Monday-through-Friday employment is pure, it's *sacred*—just as sacred as your Sunday activities.

To the pure, all things are pure.

TITUS 1:15

BIBLE READING: 1 THESSALONIANS 4:11–12; JAMES 1:14–24

MAY

-13-

How often must God prove to us that He is the Shepherd and we are the sheep . . . that He is the Vine and we are the branches, before we bow and quietly whisper, "Have Your own way, Lord"? Seems to me that if the Son of God found it necessary at the crossroad of His earthly existence to pray "not as I will, but as You will," we would be wise to use the same words often—like every day.

Not as I will, but as You will.

MATTHEW 26:39

BIBLE READING: JOHN 15:1–11

MAY

-14-

Sometimes we just don't feel like singing or smiling. Matter of fact, there are times it's hypocritical to paste a smile on your face.

It is in those times that I am most thankful for the Scriptures. In God's Word we not only discover His will for our lives, we find words of genuine comfort for those times when life comes unglued.

Blessed be . . . the Father of mercies and God
of all comfort, who comforts us in all our affliction.

2 CORINTHIANS 1:3—4

BIBLE READING: 2 CORINTHIANS 1:1—7

MAY

-15-

Acceptance is taking from God's hand absolutely anything He gives, looking into His face in trust and thanksgiving, knowing that the confinement of the hedge we're in is good and for His glory. Even though what we're enduring may be painful, it's good simply because God Himself has allowed it. Acceptance is resting in God's goodness, believing that He has all things under His control— even people who are doing what is wrong. Yes . . . even wrongdoers.

You are my hiding place; You preserve me from trouble; You surround me with songs of deliverance.

PSALM 32:7

BIBLE READING: PSALM 32, 134

CHARLES SWINDOLL

MAY
-16-

When money is our objective, we must live in fear of losing it, which makes us paranoid and suspicious. When fame is our aim, we become competitive lest others upstage us, which makes us envious. When power and influence drive us, we become self-serving and strong-willed, which makes us arrogant. And when possessions become our god, we become materialistic, thinking enough is never enough, which makes us greedy. All these pursuits fly in the face of contentment . . . and joy.

Christ will even now, as always,
be exalted in my body, whether by life or by death.

PHILIPPIANS 1:20

BIBLE READING: PROVERBS 23:4–5; 11:28; 3:9

MAY

-17-

I love Eugene Peterson's rendering of Romans 5:20 in *The Message*: "But sin . . . doesn't have a chance in competition with the aggressive forgiveness we call *grace*."

I've never met a person who truly understood and embraced grace who also continued to hold a grudge. That "aggressive forgiveness" removes the stings and replaces them with waves upon waves of gratitude to God.

Where sin increased, grace abounded all the more.

ROMANS 5:20

BIBLE READING: MATTHEW 5:44; 6:14–15; JOHN 20:23

CHARLES SWINDOLL

MAY

-18-

We have the greatest confidence in God's Spirit to provide the strength we'll need to face whatever lies ahead. Because . . .

- we have a "Helper" who has been "called alongside."
- in place of weakness, He brings power.
- in place of ignorance, He brings knowledge.
- in place of human knowledge, He brings divine wisdom and profound insights from the depths of God's plan.

Which things we also speak, not in words taught by human wisdom, but in those taught by the Spirit.

1 CORINTHIANS 2:13

BIBLE READING: JOHN 14:25–31

MAY

-19-

Thoughts are the thermostat that regulates what we accomplish in life. My body responds and reacts to the input from my mind. If I feed my mind upon doubt, disbelief, and discouragement, that is precisely the kind of day my body will experience. If I adjust my thermostat forward to thoughts filled with vision, vitality, and victory, I can count on that kind of day. You and I become what we think.

As [a man] thinks within himself, so he is.

PROVERBS 23:7

BIBLE READING: PHILIPPIANS 4:8; JEREMIAH 31:33;
MATTHEW 15:19

CHARLES SWINDOLL

MAY

-20-

The ability to get a laugh out of everyday situations is a safety valve. It rids us of tensions and worries that could otherwise damage our health.

What is it that brings healing to the emotions, healing to the soul? A joyful heart!

A joyful heart is good medicine.

PROVERBS 17:22

BIBLE READING: PSALM 126; ROMANS 15:13

MAY

-21-

We get in a hurry when we don't wait on the Lord. We jump ahead and do rash things. We shoot from the hip. We run off at the mouth, saying things that we later regret. But when we have sufficiently waited on the Lord, He gets full control of our spirit. At such moments, we're like a glove, and His hand is moving us wherever He pleases.

Rest in the LORD and wait patiently for Him.

PSALM 37:7

BIBLE READING: PSALM 37:1–11

MAY

-22-

Our mission is not to argue with those without Christ or put them down; it is to reach out to them! To model a lifestyle that is so convincing, so appealing, their curiosity will be tweaked. The non-Christian world may be lost and running on empty; but they are not stupid or unaware of their surroundings. When they come across an individual who is at peace, free of fear and worry, fulfilled, and genuinely happy, no one has to tell them that something is missing from their lives.

As You sent Me into the world,
I also have sent them into the world.

JOHN 17:18

BIBLE READING: JOHN 17:13—21

MAY

-23-

I jokingly say to people at times, "It's easier for me to know God's will for my *wife* than it is for me to know God's will for my *life*." The reality is that we often operate on that principle. We believe we know what our spouse ought to do, or what our child ought to do, or what our neighbor ought to do, or what our friend ought to do. But the tough thing is to know what I ought to be doing.

I have come . . . to do . . . the will of Him who sent Me.

JOHN 6:38

BIBLE READING: JOHN 7:1–19

CHARLES SWINDOLL

MAY
-24-

God is as much at work in the Oval Office as He is in your pastor's study. He is as much at work in the Middle East, as He is in America.

God is at work. He's moving. He's touching lives. He's shaping kingdoms. He's never surprised by what humanity may do. Just because actions or motives happen to be secular or carnal or unfair, it doesn't mean He's not present. Those involved may not be glorifying Him, but never doubt it, He's present. He's at work.

My ways [are] higher than
your ways and My thoughts than your thoughts.

ISAIAH 55:9

BIBLE READING: ISAIAH 55:6–12

MAY

-25-

When you accept Christ as the Savior and Lord of your life, the Holy Spirit comes to dwell within you. Among other things, He is there to reveal the will of God to you. Only the believer has the Spirit's presence within, and we must have this inside help if we are going to follow the will of God.

*All who are being led by the
Spirit of God, these are the sons of God.*

ROMANS 8:14

BIBLE READING: PSALM 119:1–8

CHARLES SWINDOLL

MAY

-26-

G od uses His obstacle course of faith to break through our layer of long-standing habits—those deep-seated attitudes we have formed during busy years of active service, high (often unrealistic) expectations, and success-oriented motives that only feed our carnality. All that is ultimately stripped away, and at this stage we begin to understand what God has in mind: The total renovation of our inner being. And it is here that *we learn humility*—the crowning accomplishment of God's inner working.

I was with you the whole time,
serving the Lord with all humility.

ACTS 20:19

BIBLE READING: TITUS 3:2; 1 PETER 5:5

MAY

-27-

G od has given us the privilege of choice. We can choose *for* or we can choose *against*. But we cannot choose the consequences. If we choose against the person of Jesus Christ, we thereby step into God's decree of eternal punishment. If we choose in favor of the Lord Jesus Christ, then we inherit all the rewards of heaven—the blessing of forgiven sins and eternity with God.

Do not be conformed to this world,
but be transformed by the renewing of your mind.

ROMANS 12:2

BIBLE READING: ROMANS 12:1–8

CHARLES SWINDOLL

MAY

-28-

Did you ever listen to children pray? Their faith knows no bounds. And who are the least surprised people when God answers prayer? The children.

But then we get older and grow too sophisticated for that. We use phrases like, "Let's be realistic about this." We lose that expectancy, that urgency of hope, that delightful, childlike, wide-eyed joy of faith. But God hasn't changed. He still delights in doing impossible things.

Nothing will be impossible with God.

LUKE 1:37

BIBLE READING: LUKE 1:26–38

MAY

-29-

God lives and moves outside the realm of earthly time. God has no night. God has no day. God has no month. God has no year. God has no past, present, or future. He transcends it all.

We see our life in a sequence of frames, moving from one to another, almost like a movie. Not God. He sees all the movies of our life all at once, in a flash, along with millions and billions of others going on simultaneously—past, present, and future.

Give thanks to the LORD . . .
for His lovingkindness is everlasting.

PSALM 136:1

BIBLE READING: PSALM 136:1–9

CHARLES SWINDOLL

MAY

-30-

G od's Word is a veritable storehouse of promises —over seven thousand of them. Not empty hopes and dreams, not just nice-sounding, eloquently worded thoughts that make you feel warm all over, but promises. Verbal guarantees in writing, signed by the Creator Himself.

Remember the word to Your servant,
in which You have made me hope.

PSALM 119:49

BIBLE READING: PSALM 119:33–48

MAY

-31-

"**P**ower is perfected in weakness." What an amazing statement from the Lord! And all this time we thought power was perfected in success. We've been taught all our lives that it is achievement that makes us strong. No. A thousand times, no! Those things make us proud and self-sufficient and independent. The painful thorns make us weak. But the good news is this: When we are weak, He pours His strength into us, which gives an entirely new perspective on pain and suffering, hardship and pressure.

My grace is sufficient for you, for power is perfected in weakness.

2 CORINTHIANS 12:9

BIBLE READING: 2 CORINTHIANS 12:7–21

CHARLES SWINDOLL

JUNE

God prizes generosity,
especially joyful generosity.

JUNE

-1-

Remember when Paul and Silas were seized by a hostile mob, dragged into a public marketplace, beaten mercilessly, then dumped into a dungeon with their feet fastened in stocks? As you may recall, it was around midnight at the end of that same day, while their sores were oozing and their bruises throbbing, that Paul and Silas were praying and singing a few duets of praise.

What relentless courage! What contagious joy!

*Paul and Silas were praying
and singing hymns of praise to God.*

ACTS 16:25

BIBLE READING: ACTS 16:22–31

JUNE

-2-

Listen carefully! Jesus Christ opens the gate, gently looks at you, and says: "Come to Me, all you who labor and are . . . over burdened, and I will cause you to rest."

Nothing complicated. No big fanfare, no trip to Mecca, no hypnotic trance, no fee, no special password. Just *come*. Meaning? Unload. Unhook the pack and drop it in His lap. He'll take the stress while you take a rest.

Come to Me, all you who labor and are . . .
over burdened, and I will cause you to rest—I will ease
and relieve and refresh your souls.

MATTHEW 11:28, TLB

BIBLE READING: PSALM 55:16–22

JUNE

-3-

Considering quitting? Entertaining the idea of running away . . . stopping before it's finished?

Don't! The Lord never promised you a rose garden. In fact, the only time He ever used the word "easy" was when He referred to a yoke.

Every journey is accomplished one step at a time.

Be steadfast, immovable,
always abounding in the work of the Lord.

1 CORINTHIANS 15:58

BIBLE READING: PSALM 147:1–6

CHARLES SWINDOLL

JUNE
-4-

The situation that looms in front of you may seem impossible to overcome in your own strength. It might be the result of your own actions, or you may be an innocent victim, caught in the backlash of someone else's consequences. Whatever the case, we can easily become intimidated, even fearful, and eventually immobile. The only way to move beyond that sort of paralyzing stalemate is to learn to accept and trust God's plan. You release the controls and wait for Him to move.

I delight to do Your will,
O my God; Your Law is within my heart.

PSALM 40:8

BIBLE READING: PSALM 40:1–8

JUNE

-5-

It was a glorious day when I was liberated from the fear of saying, "I don't understand why, but I accept God's hand in what has happened." It was a *greater* day when I realized that nobody expected me to have all the answers . . . least of all God! If I could figure it all out, I'd qualify as His adviser, and Scripture makes it clear He doesn't need my puny counsel. He wants my unreserved love, my unqualified devotion, my undaunted trust—not my unenlightened analysis of His ways.

But our God is in the heavens; He does whatever He pleases.

PSALM 115:3

BIBLE READING: ISAIAH 45:5—9; 46:8—11

CHARLES SWINDOLL

JUNE

-6-

You may be backed up against a set of circumstances that look pretty hopeless.

The One who directed that stone in between Goliath's eyes and split the Red Sea down the middle takes a delight in mixing up the odds.

Don't manufacture conclusions. When the Lord is in it, anything is possible.

With God all things are possible.

MATTHEW 19:26

BIBLE READING: JAMES 4:13–17; PROVERBS 19:21

JUNE

-7-

The children worked long and hard on their little cardboard shack. It was to be a special spot—a clubhouse, where they could meet together, play, and have fun. Since a clubhouse has to have rules, they came up with three:

Nobody act big.

Nobody act small.

Everybody act medium.

Not bad theology!

Give preference to one another in honor.

ROMANS 12:10

BIBLE READING: ROMANS 12:9–14

CHARLES SWINDOLL

JUNE
-8-

The criminal hanging alongside Jesus was not ushered into Paradise on the basis of anything he had done. It was God's grace that opened the door and invited him in.

Anytime you are tempted to believe in salvation-by-good-works, just remember the thief on the cross. Hopelessly lost, condemned to die by crucifixion, he says in simple faith, "Remember me." Salvation has not gotten more complicated. Simple faith is still the only way.

The Lord . . . is . . . wishing for all to come to repentance.

2 PETER 3:9

BIBLE READING: EPHESIANS 2:9; JAMES 2:14–26

JUNE

-9-

Since when is a bleeding ulcer a sign of spirituality? Or a seventy-hour week a mark of efficiency?

The world beginning to get you down? Too tired to pray? Let me suggest one of the few four-letter words God loves to hear us shout:

HELP!

My God will supply all your needs
according to His riches in glory in Christ Jesus.

PHILIPPIANS 4:19

BIBLE READING: PHILIPPIANS 2:19–30; 4:2–3

JUNE

-10-

"What is man, that You take thought of him?" What a great question!

In a world consumed with thoughts of itself, filled with people impressed with each other, having disconnected with the only One worthy of praise, it's time we return to Theology 101 and sit silently in His presence. It's time we catch a fresh glimpse of Him who, alone, is awesome. He is our infinite, inexhaustible God. The one we worship defies human analysis.

What is man, that You take thought of him?

PSALM 8:4

BIBLE READING: PSALM 8; 9:1—6

JUNE
-11-

As soon as we walk across that stage and receive that diploma, we're ready for the big time. Our slick resume makes us look like a combination of Joan of Arc, Winston Churchill, and Mother Theresa.

But that's not God's way. He prepares His servants most often through extended periods of waiting, designed to hone skills and break wills, to shape character and give depth.

With Your counsel You will guide me,
and afterward receive me to glory.

PSALM 73:24

BIBLE READING: PSALM 78:1–8

CHARLES SWINDOLL

JUNE
-12-

We continually encounter hardships. People disappoint us. We disappoint ourselves. But God is constant and compassionate. We are not alone. He cares. Against all reason, the transcendent God loves us so much that He has committed Himself to us. That's why Paul could proclaim:

Neither death, nor life, nor angels, nor principalities,
nor things present, nor things to come,
nor powers, nor height, nor depth, nor any other
created thing, shall be able to separate us
from the love of God, which is in Christ Jesus our Lord.

ROMANS 8:38–39

BIBLE READING: PSALM 103

JUNE

-13-

The Lord is a master at taking our turmoil and revealing the best possible solution to us.

As Peter once wrote: "casting all your anxiety upon Him because He cares for you."

When we do that, He trades us His joy for our anxiety. *Such a deal!* As He then works things out and makes it clear to us which step to take next, we can relax, release the tension, and laugh again.

Humble yourselves under the might hand of God, that He may exalt you at the proper time, casting all your anxiety upon Him because He cares for you.

1 PETER 5:6–7

BIBLE READING: 1 PETER 5:1–11

CHARLES SWINDOLL

JUNE
-14-

Why was Joseph considered great? He certainly wasn't superhuman. He never walked on water. He had no halo.

Then, why was Joseph so great? He was great because of his faith in God, which manifested itself in a magnanimous attitude toward others and his magnificent attitude toward difficulties. A strong faith leads to a good attitude.

The arms of his hands were made
strong by the hands of the Mighty God of Jacob.

GENESIS 49:24, TLB

BIBLE READING: GENESIS 45:1–8

JUNE

-15-

When the Lord delivered your salvation, His Spirit came within you as part of the package deal. The Spirit of God took up permanent residence within you. And when He entered your life, He brought with Him—for you—the full capacity of His power. Without Christ, you and I were like a vast, empty reservoir awaiting the coming of a downpour. As salvation became a reality, this emptiness became full to the point of running over. The Spirit of God has filled our internal capacity with power and dynamic.

Be filled with the Spirit.

Ephesians 5:18

Bible Reading: Ephesians 6:10–24

CHARLES SWINDOLL

JUNE
-16-

Many of God's servants are simply too serious! Leaders must have the ability to take criticism, and they must have the ability to laugh at themselves.

Equally important, of course, is the ability to sift from any criticism what is actually true. We are foolish if we respond angrily to every criticism. Who knows, God may be using those very words to teach us some essential lessons, painful though they may be.

Better is open rebuke than love that is concealed.

PROVERBS 27:5

BIBLE READING: PROVERBS 27:5–11

JUNE
-17-

Through it *all*. That's the ticket. Through the victories and the failures. . . . Through the brilliant days of accomplishment and the broken days. . . . Through the heady days of laughter and success and those nameless intervals of setback and blank despair. Through it all, God is with us, leading us, teaching us, humbling us, preparing us.

I will say to the LORD, "My refuge
and my fortress, my God, in whom I trust."

PSALM 91:2

BIBLE READING: EPHESIANS 1:18–19; ISAIAH 58:11

CHARLES SWINDOLL

JUNE
-18-

Having been swamped by sin all our lives, struggling to find our way to the top of the water to breathe, we can find great hope in the ability God gives us not only to breathe but to swim freely. You see, Christ not only lived an exemplary life, He also makes it possible for us to do the same. He gives us His pattern to follow without while at the same time providing the needed power within.

He who began a good work in you
will perfect it until the day of Christ Jesus.

PHILIPPIANS 1:6

BIBLE READING: PHILIPPIANS 1:1—11;
2 CORINTHIANS 12:7—12

JUNE
-19-

Webster defines hope, "to desire with expectation of fulfillment." To hope is to anticipate. It is more than dreaming, however. It is possessing within ourselves an expectation that someday there will be the fulfillment of that desire. It will become a reality. Hope always looks to the future, it's always on tiptoes. It keeps us going. It makes a dismal today bearable because it promises a brighter tomorrow.

The way of the LORD is a stronghold to
the upright. . . . The righteous will never be shaken.

PROVERBS 10:29–30

BIBLE READING: PSALM 65

CHARLES SWINDOLL

JUNE
-20-

The returning prodigal was amazed by his father's immediate acceptance, reckless forgiveness, and unconditional love. Having been so distant, so desperate, so utterly alone, he knew no way to turn but homeward. Then, at the end of his rope, he found himself suddenly safe in his dad's embrace, surrounded by extravagant grace.

Every day God says to our world, "All is forgiven . . . come on home." His arms are open, and there is a smile on His face. All that is needed is you.

You sins have been forgiven you for His name's sake.

1 JOHN 2:12

BIBLE READING: 1 JOHN 2:1–14

JUNE

-21-

Job speaks of the One who "commands the sun not to shine, and sets a seal on the stars." We can set our watches by these heavenly lights God put in motion. He does "great things," says Job, things that are "unfathomable." When it comes to God's workings and plans, we will never be able to say, "Finally, I've figured it all out!"—not until we get to heaven, when we will know as we are known.

Who commands the sun
not to shine, and sets a seal upon the stars.

JOB 9:7

BIBLE READING: JOB 9:1–12

JUNE
-22-

History is full of individuals who made a difference. Think of Michelangelo, Brahms, and Beethoven. Think of the scientists and explorers who have changed the course of history. Think of the courageous preachers who have stood alone in the gap and made a difference.

From Genesis to Revelation, we see God's hand on the lives of individuals who thought and said and did what was right—regardless—and as a result, history was made.

I searched for a man . . .
who would . . . stand in the gap.

E z e k i e l   2 2 : 3 0

Bible Reading: 2 Chronicles 16:9; Jeremiah 5:1

JUNE
-23-

Change, for most folks, is enormously challenging. Everything within us screams, "Just leave it alone. If it ain't broke, don't fix it." But sometimes things need to be rearranged even though they aren't broken. Sometimes we need a major change of direction—not because we are necessarily going in an evil direction, it's just not the direction God wants for us. God does not want us to substitute the good for the very best.

The refining pot is for silver and
the furnace for gold, but the LORD tests hearts.

PROVERBS 17:3

BIBLE READING: GALATIANS 2:16, 21; 1 JOHN 2:3–6

CHARLES SWINDOLL

JUNE
-24-

Expressing emotions is not a mark of immaturity or carnality. The loss of a loved one is just as much a loss for the believer as it is for the non-believer. A killer disease like cancer—especially in its final stages—arouses the same feelings in the Christian's heart as in the heart without Christ. Pain is pain. Loss is loss. Death is death. At such times tears are not only acceptable, they are appropriate and expected. It is part of being real, being human. Nothing is gained by denial or proven by remaining stoic.

Rejoice with those who rejoice, and weep with those who weep.

ROMANS 12:15

BIBLE READING: PSALM 142

JUNE
-25-

If you walk with the Lord long enough, you will discover that His tests often come back-to-back. As soon as you climb out of one crucible, thinking, *Okay, I made it through that one,* you're plunged into another one.

Crucibles create Christlikeness.

The work of righteousness will be peace, and the service of righteousness, quietness and confidence forever.

ISAIAH 32:17

BIBLE READING: 1 CORINTHIANS 4:1–7

JUNE

-26-

God rules. God reigns. God, and God alone. And His way is right. It leads to His glory.

Deep within the hearts of men and women, even though most would never acknowledge it, is this realization that we really don't have the final answer.

The Son Himself also will be subjected to the One who subjected all things to Him, that God may be all in all.

1 CORINTHIANS 15:28

BIBLE READING: 1 CORINTHIANS 15:20–28

JUNE
-27-

We fall in love with the gifts, rather that the Giver.

God gives us a loving wife or husband or friend, and we fall more in love with the person than the One who gave us that individual. God gives us a good job, and we love the job more than we love Him. And All the while He stands at the window and says, "Look up here. I gave that to you." He longs to have us look up and say, "Oh, thank You, Father! I miss You. I want to be with You."

Turn to Me, and be saved, all you ends of the earth!

ISAIAH 45:22, NKJV

BIBLE READING: ISAIAH 45:14—25

CHARLES SWINDOLL

JUNE

-28-

Our final home is not planet earth. Our future is sure. In the meantime, God is in control. Make that in *full* control.

The literal rendering of Psalm 46:1 goes something like this: "God is our refuge and strength; abundantly available for help in tight places."

In a tight place? Don't fear. You are right where He wants you.

God is our refuge and strength, a very present help in trouble.

PSALMS 46:1

BIBLE READING: PSALM 46

JUNE

-29-

God deals with the hard questions of life. Not questions like how do I make a living, but how do I make a life? Not how do I spend my time, but how do I spend eternity? And not so much how do I get along with the person who sits next to me, but ultimately, how do I get along with God? When we answer the hard questions correctly, all the others fall into place.

Behold, God is my salvation, I will trust and not be afraid.

ISAIAH 12:2

BIBLE READING: ROMANS 8:26–31

CHARLES SWINDOLL

JUNE
-30-

"Father, forgive them for they don't know what they are doing." Jesus managed to utter those penetrating words through bleeding, cracked lips, swollen from the noonday sun. Impaled on that cruel, Roman cross, He interceded on behalf of His enemies. What a magnificent model of forgiveness!

He paid the penalty in full for the sins of the world, the just for the unjust. He's our model for correctly resolving disputes. Ultimately, it's a matter of forgiveness.

"Father, forgive them; for they do not know what they are doing."

LUKE 23:34

BIBLE READING: MATTHEW 6:14–15; LUKE 17:3–4

JULY

GOD'S TIMING IS

ALWAYS ON TIME.

JULY

-1-

God's redemptive providence is always at work, even through the most diabolical schemes and actions. Classic illustration? The betrayal of Jesus Christ by Judas. Strange as it may seem, Judas' worst act of wickedness helped to bring about the best thing that ever happened: the Atonement.

So, take heart, my friend. Nothing is happening on earth that brings a surprise to heaven. Nothing!

"You meant evil against me, but God meant it for good."

GENESIS 50:20

BIBLE READING: GENESIS 50

JULY

-2-

The traits we remember and admire most about David were shaped while he lived like a fugitive in the wilderness. Great character, like massive roots, grows deep when water is sparse and winds are strong, and the psalms we turn to, most often emerged from a broken heart while tears wouldn't stop and questions remained unanswered.

Some of your best traits and some of your finest works will grow out of the incredibly painful periods in your life.

I shall offer a sacrifice of thanksgiving.
And call upon the name of the LORD.

PSALM 116:17

BIBLE READING: PSALM 116:12–19

JULY

-3-

We need to forgive. But forgiving goes against all the stuff your old nature wants to see happen. Everything within you screams, "Get back . . . get even!" As logical as that seems, however, those are the very sounds of misery that fill the torture chamber of an unforgiving heart.

We are most like beasts when we kill. We are most like men when we judge. We are most like God when we forgive.

Blessed are the merciful, for they shall receive mercy.

MATTHEW 5:7

BIBLE READING: MATTHEW 18:21–35

CHARLES SWINDOLL

JULY

-4-

"*o not fear. When you pass through the waters, I will be with you.*" Isaiah was not writing of literal waters or actual rivers. His figure of speech emphasized encroaching circumstances that threatened the stability of one's faith. When the waters rise to dangerous depths, when difficulties reach maximum proportion, when your ship seems to be disintegrating board by board and starting to sink by life's inevitable storms, *God is faithful*. He promises, "I will be with you."

When you pass through the waters, I will be with you.

ISAIAH 43:2

BIBLE READING: ISAIAH 43:1–7

JULY

-5-

It's hard to have dreams dashed, to have hopes unfulfilled, to face a future that is unknown and unfamiliar and sometimes, if the truth were known, unwanted. But God has a way of guiding us unerringly into the path of righteousness for His name's sake.

Isn't it about time you stopped trying to figure it all out? Then let it be, my friend . . . let it be.

He guides me in the paths of righteousness for His name's sake.

PSALM 23:3

BIBLE READING: PSALM 89:1–10

JULY

-6-

I firmly believe God's Word has been preserved, not merely as a collection of historical documents and geographical studies, but as a trustworthy resource—a place we turn to for assistance in living our lives in ways that honor Christ.

In the pages of Scripture, God has given us models—people, believe it or not, who are just like you and me, who, despite the odds, lived lives pleasing to Him. By faith. In obedience. With courage.

You are my hiding place and my shield; I wait for Your word.

PSALM 119:114

BIBLE READING: PSALM 119:113–120

JULY

- 7 -

Restraining ourselves—self-control—is so important that God lists it as a fruit of the Spirit.

Removing restraint from your life may seem like an exciting adventure, but it inevitably leads to tragedy. It's a lot like removing the brakes from your car. That may be daring and filled with thrills for awhile, but injury is certain. Take away the brakes and your life, like your car, is transformed into an unguided missile—destined for disaster.

The fruit of the Spirit is . . . self-control.

GALATIANS 5 : 2 2 − 2 3

BIBLE READING: PROVERBS 17:14, 28; 22:24−25; 29:11

CHARLES SWINDOLL

JULY

- 8 -

You may have lived a life as blatantly sinful as the thug hanging beside Jesus on the cross or you may have lived a good and respectable life. It makes no difference. We all approach the throne of God as sinners, and we all are saved by His grace alone.

I am the way, and the truth, and the life;
no one comes to the Father, but through Me.

JOHN 14:6

BIBLE READING: JOHN 10:1–21

JULY

-9-

Let's be thankful for angels—those unseen guardians who work overtime, who never slumber or sleep. Think of all the accidents they have prevented, all the little kids they have protected, all the enemy assaults they have resisted.

The Scriptures speak very clearly of the angels. They are frequently dispatched to earth in human form to bring encouragement and assistance.

He will give His angels charge
concerning you, to guard you in all your ways.

PSALM 91:11

BIBLE READING: Psalm 91:11–16; Hebrews 13:2

CHARLES SWINDOLL

JULY
-10-

Rather than racing into the limelight, we need to accept our role in the shadows. Don't promote yourself. Don't push yourself to the front. Let someone else do that. Better yet, let God do that.

If you're great, trust me, the word will get out. You'll be found . . . in God's time. If you're necessary for the plan, God will put you in the right place at just the precise time.

Wait for the LORD; be strong and let
your heart take courage; yes, wait for the LORD.

PSALM 27:14

BIBLE READING: PSALM 27:7–14; JAMES 4:13–17

JULY
-11-

Worried about your kids?
Leave it to God.
Living in a place you'd rather not be?
Leave it to God.
Looks like you won't graduate with honors?
Leave it to God.
You did the job but someone else got the credit?
Leave it to God.

O my God, in You I trust.

PSALM 25:2

BIBLE READING: PSALM 23, 25

CHARLES SWINDOLL

JULY

-12-

To be "humble in heart" is to be more interested in serving the needs of others than in having one's own needs met:

- When a husband is unselfish, he subjugates his own wants and desires to the needs of his wife and family.
- When a mother is unselfish, she isn't irked by having to give up her agenda for the sake of her children.

Take my yoke upon you, and learn from Me,
for I am gentle and humble in heart.

MATTHEW 11:29

BIBLE READING: MATTHEW 16:24–28

JULY

-13-

The only way to find happiness in the grind of life is *by faith*. A faith-filled life means all the difference in how we view everything around us. It affects our attitudes toward people, toward circumstances, toward ourselves. Only then do our feet become swift to do what is right.

You say you want to be considered great some day? Here's the secret: Walk by faith, trusting God to renew your attitude.

Be steadfast, immovable,
always abounding in the work of the Lord.

1 CORINTHIANS 15:58

BIBLE READING: HEBREWS 11:1, 6; JAMES 2:14–17

CHARLES SWINDOLL

JULY

-14-

When God created humanity, He put something of Himself in each of us. Unlike the beasts of the field or the birds of the sky, He placed within us His "image."

That "image" sets human beings apart from all other living things on earth. With body, soul, and spirit, we are able to get in touch not only with our feelings, but with Him, our Creator. And, equally important, He is able to communicate with us.

God created man in His
own image, in the image of God He created him.

GENESIS 1:27

BIBLE READING: GENESIS 1:27–2:25

JULY

-15-

Godliness is something below the surface of a life, deep down in the realm of attitude . . . an attitude toward God Himself.

The longer I think about this, the more I believe that a person who is godly is one whose heart is sensitive toward God, one who takes God seriously. This evidences itself in one very obvious mannerism: the godly individual hungers and thirsts after God.

As the deer pants for the water brooks,
so my soul pants for You, O God.

PSALM 42:1

BIBLE READING: PSALM 42

CHARLES SWINDOLL

JULY

-16-

"I accept you as you are."

"I believe you are valuable."

"I care when you hurt."

"I desire only what is best for you."

"I erase all offenses."

We could call that the ABC's of love. And I don't know of anybody who would turn his back on such magnetic, encouraging statements.

The whole Law is fulfilled in
one word; . . . "You shall love your neighbor as yourself."

GALATIANS 5:14

BIBLE READING: 1 JOHN 3

JULY

-17-

God can use our authority and our abundance and our promotion. But before He can, we need to humble ourselves before God's mighty hand and say, "Jesus Christ, I need You. I have all of this to account for, and I can't take any of it with me. Please use me as you see fit." With authority comes the need for accountability. With popularity comes the need for humility. With prosperity comes the need for integrity.

I dwell . . . with the lowly and contrite of spirit.

ISAIAH 57:15

BIBLE READING: ROMANS 2:1–8

CHARLES SWINDOLL

JULY

-18-

Maybe you have found yourself suddenly face-to-face with a situation that, a year ago, you would never have dreamed could be true in your life . . . but now it is. God is "pressing" you in the midst of your own Gethsemane, saying, "I want to have My will in your life. I want you to release your rights. I want you to be willing to accept My will."

Not my will but yours be done.

LUKE 22:42

BIBLE READING: MATTHEW 6:20; JOHN 5:30; HEBREWS 10:9

JULY

-19-

Rigid love is not true love. It is veiled manipulation, a conditional time bomb that explodes when frustrated. Genuine love willingly waits! It isn't pushy or demanding. While it has its limits, its boundaries are far-reaching. It neither clutches nor clings. Real love is not shortsighted, selfish, or insensitive. It detects needs and does what is best for the other person without being told.

God is love, and he who abides
in love abides in God, and God abides in him.

1 JOHN 4:16

BIBLE READING: 1 JOHN 4:7–21

CHARLES SWINDOLL

JULY

-20-

By making us in His image, God gave us capacities not given to other forms of life. Ideally, He made us to know Him, to love Him, and to obey Him. He did not put rings in our noses to pull us around like oxen, nor did He create us with strings permanently attached to our hands and feet like human marionettes.

No, He gave us freedom to make choices.

Who is the man who fears the LORD?
He will instruct him in the way he should choose.

PSALM 25:12

BIBLE READING: PSALM 25:1–11

JULY
-21-

I sn't God the One who urges us to "Make a joyful noise unto the Lord"? Why do we always think that means singing? Seems to me that the most obvious joyful noise on earth is laughter.

We all *look* so much better and *feel* so much better when we laugh. I don't know of a more contagious sound.

Shout joyfully to the LORD, all the earth.

PSALM 100:1

BIBLE READING: PSALM 100

CHARLES SWINDOLL

JULY

-22-

So many things that happen in this life are past searching out. I can't explain God's plan. I can only verify from Scripture how unfathomable it is.

Before I ever have a thought, God knows it's on its way. He knows when it strikes my brain and what's going to come as a result of it. Yet I still have the freedom to think that thought and follow through on that action. This is part of the unfathomable nature of God.

You understand my thought from afar
. . . and are intimately acquainted with all my ways.

PSALM 139:2–3

BIBLE READING: PSALM 94:11; PROVERBS 16:3; ISAIAH 55:8

JULY
-23-

In our overpopulated world, it is easy to underestimate the significance of one. It is easy to underestimate the value of you: your vote, your convictions, your determination to say, "I stand against this."

Does it matter if we get involved or not? It matters greatly—it matters to your character!

> *"Who knows whether you have*
> *not attained royalty for such a time as this?"*
>
> ESTHER 4:14

BIBLE READING: ESTHER 4; 9:20—32

CHARLES SWINDOLL

JULY

-24-

At the fork of every road, we need faith and action to follow God's leading. It's a turning point, where we must make a decision. It's like those expressway signs that say "Garden Grove Freeway, East, West," with arrows pointing to the two exit lanes. You're rolling along carefree at sixty-five miles an hour and suddenly you have to decide. Which way? Only one way will get you where you want to go. So you have to make a decision. You can try to go in both directions but it won't work.

All the paths of the LORD are
lovingkindness and truth to those who keep His covenant.

PSALM 25:10

BIBLE READING: EPHESIANS 5:10; PHILIPPIANS 2:12—13

JULY

-25-

The apostle Paul did not write that Christians are not to grieve, but that we do not grieve as if we "have no hope." There should be a lot of room in our theology for feelings of loss and tears, just as there is room for lighthearted, joyous feelings and great laughter. The Spirit of God prompts both.

You will not grieve as do the rest who have no hope.

1 THESSALONIANS 4:13

BIBLE READING: 1 THESSALONIANS 4:13–18

G od knows where we are going tomorrow, next week, and next year. That's something we don't know. And I, for one, am so glad I don't. If right now I knew everything that faced me in the coming year, I would be scared to the point of sleeplessness. But God knows. How gracious of Him to lead us one step at a time.

*Trust in the LORD with all your heart
and do not lean on your own understanding.*

PROVERBS 3:5

BIBLE READING: PROVERBS 3:1—7

JULY

-27-

God's Word makes you and me wiser than our enemies, gives us more insight than we had from our teachers, and provides us an understanding that's beyond the aged. That's an awfully good set of promises.

Your word is a lamp to my feet, and a light to my path.

PSALM 119:105

BIBLE READING: PSALM 119:9–16

CHARLES SWINDOLL

JULY

-28-

God is good! How full of compassion He is! We find great comfort in this.

God is also just. In the Scriptures His justice and righteousness are intertwined. In fact, the same original term in the sacred text is often translated either "justice" or "righteousness." We love the fact that God is good and compassionate, but it doesn't sit with us quite as easily that He is just.

All His ways are just, . . . righteous and upright is He.

DEUTERONOMY 32:4

BIBLE READING: DEUTERONOMY 32:1–6, 36–43

JULY

-29-

I have two enduring goals in life. First and foremost, *I desire to learn how to think biblically.* I want to see life through the lens of God's eyes. I don't want to argue with Him, I don't want to fight Him, I don't even need to understand Him, but I desperately desire to obey Him. And so I want to see life, whether it be struggle or joy, through God's perspective.

And coming in a close second, I want to encourage other people to do the same thing.

Fixing our eyes on Jesus, the author and perfecter of faith.

HEBREWS 12:2

BIBLE READING: HEBREWS 12:4—17

CHARLES SWINDOLL

JULY

-30-

When God forgives, He forgets. He is not only willing but pleased to use any vessel— just as long as it is clean today. It may be cracked or chipped. It may be worn. But you can count on this—the past ended one second ago. From this point onward, you can be clean, filled with His Spirit, and used for His honor.

You will cast all their sins into the depths of the sea.

MICAH 7:19

BIBLE READING: MICAH 7:7–20

JULY

-31-

After the final Passover meal in the upper room, Jesus led His disciples out into a dark night to face the brutal, hostile world that was waiting to condemn Him to death.

Jesus could not pay for our sin by hiding in the safety of the upper room, and we cannot remain in the safety of the sanctuary. We must go out into the world, where the presence of Jesus Christ in our lives will create in us an ability to be unique even in a hostile, desperate world.

You are the light of the world.

MATTHEW 5:14

BIBLE READING: MATTHEW 5:13–20

CHARLES SWINDOLL

AUGUST

LIFE IS NOT ABOUT YOU.

IT'S ABOUT GOD.

AUGUST

-1-

O urs is a winner-oriented world. Whether it's sports or politics, education or sales, winning is essential for survival. Seems so logical. But isn't it strange that the best lessons are invariably learned from defeat? Pain remains a strict but faithful teacher. We know that theoretically, but Job's question—"Shall we indeed accept good from God and not accept adversity?"—continues to get "No" for an answer. It seems it will take a lifetime to say "Yes"!

> *"Shall we indeed accept good
> from God and not accept adversity?"*

JOB 2:10

BIBLE READING: ROMANS 8:18–27

CHARLES SWINDOLL

AUGUST

-2-

Alone with Jethro's flock on the backside of the desert, perhaps after the howling night winds of the wilderness had settled and the searing rays of Sinai's sun began to peek over the slopes of Horeb, God spoke to Moses from the midst of a bush that remained strangely ablaze. Never again in all of time has the voice of God been heard from a bush that refused to be consumed with flames.

But never doubt it: God still longs to speak to waiting hearts . . . hearts that are quiet before Him.

"My people shall know My name; therefore in that day I am the one who is speaking, 'Here I am.'"

ISAIAH 52:6

BIBLE READING: MATTHEW 13:1–9, 18–23

AUGUST

-3-

No one wants to be shipwrecked. But the reality is, it happens, not only on the open sea, but also in life.

The secret of survival is what you do ahead of time in calmer waters. If your life is storm-free as you read this book, I urge you to take advantage of the peaceful lull. Spend time in God's Word. Deepen your walk with Him through prayer and personal worship. Then, when the inevitable winds of adversity begin to blow you'll be ready to respond in faith, rather than fear.

When I am afraid, I will put my trust in You.

PSALM 56:3

BIBLE READING: ACTS 27:41–44; PSALM 56

CHARLES SWINDOLL

AUGUST

-4-

G od, our wise and creative Maker, has been pleased to make everyone different and no one perfect. The sooner we appreciate and accept that fact, the deeper we will appreciate and accept one another, just as our Designer planned us. Actually, there is only one thing that would be worse than constant comparison, and that is if everyone were just alike.

That's a frightening thought!

We do not dare to classify or compare ourselves.

2 CORINTHIANS 10:12, NIV

BIBLE READING: 2 CORINTHIANS 10:1–18; GALATIANS 6:1–5

AUGUST

-5-

I have found great help from two truths God gave me at a time in my life when I was bombarded with a series of unexpected and unfair blows (from my perspective).

First, *nothing touches me that has not passed through the hands of my heavenly Father.*

Second, *everything I endure is designed to prepare me for serving others more effectively.*

*Momentary, light affliction is
producing for us an eternal weight of glory.*

2 CORINTHIANS 4:17

BIBLE READING: 2 CORINTHIANS 4

CHARLES SWINDOLL

AUGUST

-6-

Christ offered Himself as a sacrifice for our sins, once for all. Never again would the priest have to make sacrifices in the Temple; never again would blood have to be shed for the forgiveness of sins. Christ was God's one, final, acceptable sacrifice. Mission accomplished! Having made that sacrifice, Christ satisfied the Father's demand on sin and opened the way for us to know God intimately.

*Jesus has entered as a forerunner
for us, having become a high priest forever.*

HEBREWS 6:20

BIBLE READING: HEBREWS 7

AUGUST

-7-

Two ears. Two eyes. Only one mouth. Maybe that should tell us something. I challenge you to join me in becoming a better listener. With your mate. Your kids. Your boss. Your clients. Your fellow Christians as well as those who need to meet Christ.

What does it take? Several things. Rare qualities. Like caring. Time. Unselfishness. Concentration. Holding the other person in high esteem.

The hearing ear and the
seeing eye, the LORD has made both of them.

PROVERBS 20:12

BIBLE READING: LUKE 8:4–18; JAMES 1:19

CHARLES SWINDOLL

AUGUST

-8-

I'll let you in on a secret: Living and learning go hand in hand. Remember Caleb? He was eighty-five and still growing when he grabbed the challenge of the future. At a time when the ease and comfort of retirement seemed predictable, he fearlessly faced the invincible giants of the mountain. There was no dust on that fella. Every new sunrise introduced another reminder that his body and a rocking chair weren't made for each other.

May the God of peace . . . make you
complete in every good work to do His will.

HEBREWS 13:20–21, NKJV

BIBLE READING: JOSHUA 14

AUGUST

-9-

God's goal is not to make sure you're happy. No matter how hard it is for you to believe this, it's time to do so. Life is not about your being comfortable and happy and successful and pain free. It's about becoming the man or woman God has called you to be.

Life is not about *you!* It's about *God.*

Our old self was crucified with Him,
in order that our body of sin might be done away with.

ROMANS 6:6

BIBLE READING: ROMANS 6:1—11

CHARLES SWINDOLL

AUGUST

-10-

When will we ever learn that there are no hopeless situations, only people who have grown hopeless about them? What appears as an unsolvable problem to us is actually a rather exhilarating challenge. People who inspire others are those who see invisible bridges at the end of dead-end streets.

Stand firm in the Lord.

PHILIPPIANS 4:1

BIBLE READING: PHILIPPIANS 4:6–9

AUGUST

-11-

Every aspect of Jesus' becoming human began with an attitude of submission. Rather than lobbying for His right to remain in heaven and continuing to enjoy all the benefits of that exalted role as the second member of the Godhead and Lord of the created world, He willingly said yes. He agreed to cooperate with a plan that would require His releasing ecstasy and accepting agony.

Being found in appearance as a man,
He humbled Himself by
becoming obedient to the point of death.

PHILIPPIANS 2:8

BIBLE READING: MATTHEW 19:16–26

CHARLES SWINDOLL

AUGUST

-12-

Someone said, "Business is a lot like the game of tennis. Those who don't serve well end up losing."

Do you serve under someone else's authority? How's your attitude, toward that person? Having the right attitude can be especially tough if the person to whom you answer is a difficult individual or an incompetent leader or one whose weaknesses you know all too well. This is not only a test of your loyalty, but a test of your Christian maturity.

Even if you should suffer
for the sake of righteousness, you are blessed.

1 PETER 3:14

BIBLE READING: HEBREWS 13:7; 1 PETER 5:5–6

AUGUST

-13-

Some of the most profound ministries of the Spirit of God are not public or loud or large. Sometimes His most meaningful touch on our lives comes when we are all alone.

Sometimes just being alone out in God's marvelous creation is all that's needed for the scales to be removed from your eyes and for you to begin to hear from God.

He will be quiet in His love, He will rejoice over you.

ZEPHANIAH 3:17

BIBLE READING: 1 KINGS 19:9–13

CHARLES SWINDOLL

AUGUST

-14-

Every achievement worth remembering is stained with the blood of diligence and scarred by the wounds of disappointment. To quit, to run, to escape, to hide—none of these options solve anything. They only postpone reckoning with reality.

Every journey is accomplished one step at a time. Don't stop now!

Continue in the faith firmly established and steadfast.

COLOSSIANS 1:23

BIBLE READING: 2 PETER 3:1–9

AUGUST

-15-

Only Christ can satisfy, whether we have or don't have, whether we are known or unknown, whether we live or die. . . . The pursuit of happiness is the cultivation of a Christ-centered, Christ-controlled life.

To me, to live is Christ and to die is gain.

PHILIPPIANS 1:21

BIBLE READING: PHILIPPIANS 1:12–26

CHARLES SWINDOLL

AUGUST

-16-

In the cross, the Lord God arranged a plan for our spiritual survival with divine integrity. It required the sacrifice of Christ on the cross. He followed through. We can take Him at His word. He was who He said He was, and He did what He said He would do. With a single heart and a single mind and a single will, He fulfilled the Father's plan.

I came that they may have life, and have it abundantly.

JOHN 10:10

BIBLE READING: ROMANS 6:1—23

AUGUST

-17-

G od is the Potter, we are the clay. He is the one who gives the commands; we are the ones who obey. He never has to explain Himself; He never has to ask permission. He is shaping us over into the image of His Son, regardless of the pain and heartache that may require. Those lessons are learned a little easier when we remember that we are not in charge, He is.

You are our Father; we are the clay, and You our potter; and all of us are the work of Your hand.

ISAIAH 64:8

BIBLE READING: ISAIAH 40:28—29

CHARLES SWINDOLL

AUGUST

-18-

No matter how bad things seem, deliberately letting your mind dwell on positive, thoughts will enable you to survive.

I frequently quote Philippians 4:8 to myself. I say, "Okay, Chuck, it's time to let your mind dwell on better things." And then I go over the list and deliberately replace a worry with something honorable or pure or lovely, something worthy of praise. It never fails—the pressure begins to fade and peace begins to emerge.

Whatever is true, whatever is honorable, whatever is right, . . . let your mind dwell on these things.

PHILIPPIANS 4:8

BIBLE READING: ISAIAH 55:6–13

AUGUST
-19-

It may seem to many that the One who made us is too far removed to concern Himself with the tiny details of life on this old globe. But that is not the case. His mysterious plan is running its course right on schedule, exactly as He decreed it.

This world is not out of control, spinning wildly through space. When God created the world, He also established the course of this world and His plan for humanity.

I know the plans I have for you . . .
plans . . . to give you a future and a hope.

JEREMIAH 29:11

BIBLE READING: JEREMIAH 29:10–14

CHARLES SWINDOLL

AUGUST

-20-

Y ou are a thinking citizen, an individual who knows Christ—OK, then, *do something about it!* Say something about it! Stand alone!

The question is not simply, what do you think of Christ? The question is, what have you *done* about what you think? The issue is not so much, how do you feel about the message of the gospel? The issue is, what have you done about the gospel?

You shall be My witnesses . . .
even to the remotest part of the earth.

ACTS 1:8

BIBLE READING: ACTS 1:1–8; 2:37–47

AUGUST
-21-

Faith is believing God is who He says He is and that He will do what He says He will do. Faith is obeying the Lord when I'm unsure of the outcome. Faith is trusting Him when everything in me screams for empirical proof: "Show it to me. Give me the evidence."

God wants us to walk by faith, not by sight.

He who comes to God must believe that He is,
and that He is a rewarder of those who seek Him.

HEBREWS 11:6

BIBLE READING: HEBREWS 11:8—16

AUGUST

-22-

God gave you a mind. Use it to know Him better.

God gave you a will. Use it to obey Him.

And God gave you emotions. Don't be afraid of them. Let them out. Allow your heart to show through.

Let everything that has breath praise the LORD.

PSALM 150:6

BIBLE READING: PSALM 150:1–6

AUGUST

-23-

God's provisions are often just enough; don't fail to thank Him. Maybe you don't have the job you wanted, but you do have a job. Maybe you don't have the position you planned on, but His provisions are enough . . . just enough. If you postpone your gratitude until all your dreams are fulfilled, you could easily turn into a cranky Christian, always waiting for more. Grateful contentment is a much-needed virtue in this consumptive culture.

Let us come before His presence with thanksgiving. Let us shout joyfully to Him with psalms.

PSALM 95:2

BIBLE READING: PSALM 96

CHARLES SWINDOLL

AUGUST

-24-

In searching God's Word for His will, find the subject that is closest to your area of need. Marriage, suffering, money, occupation . . . there are hundreds of subjects.

God's Word answers most of our questions, but to find those answers takes time, patience, and effort. It's like a handbook or a manual of instruction for your computer software. You may have to dig to find the answers, but they are there.

I shall delight in Your statutes; I shall not forget Your word.

PSALM 119:16

BIBLE READING: PSALM 119:17–24

AUGUST

-25-

Tennyson said: *Our echoes roll from soul to soul and grow forever and forever.*

The law of echoes applies to a marriage. You want a wife who is gracious, forgiving, tolerant, and supportive? Start with her husband! It will roll from your soul to hers, my friend!

The law of echoes applies to our work as well. Want your associates at work to be cheery and unselfish? The place to begin is with that person who stares back at you from the bathroom mirror every morning.

It is You who blesses the righteous man, O Lord.

PSALM 5:12

BIBLE READING: PSALM 5

CHARLES SWINDOLL

AUGUST
-26-

My car has warning lights on the dashboard. Every once in a while when I am driving, one of them flashes bright red. When it does, I stop and turn the engine off.

God has His own warning lights, and at times He flashes them, saying to us, "Stop, stop, don't, don't!" And if we're wise, we stop. We use the necessary disciplines that keep our minds pure, and He does His part in honoring that obedience.

If anyone is in Christ he is a new creature.

2 CORINTHIANS 5:17

BIBLE READING: 2 CORINTHIANS 5:16–21

AUGUST

-27-

You and I are locked in a tiny space on this foggy lake of life called the present. Because our entire perspective is based on this moment, we speak of the present, the past, and the future.

How do we live our lives in this little space, not knowing where the shore is—especially during the times when we do not hear God's reassuring voice? We do it by discovering how God works, by having confidence in Him.

Our help is in the name
of the LORD who made heaven and earth.

PSALM 124:8

BIBLE READING: PSALM 124; 125

AUGUST

-28-

We hardly need the reminder that the Christian life is not a cloud-nine utopia. Thinking that Christ helps you live happily ever after is downright unbiblical! Once we're in heaven, sure, that's a different story. But until then, there are not many days you could write in your journal as fantastic or incredible. Most of life is learning and growing, falling and getting back up, forgiving and forgetting, accepting and going on.

Teach me to do Your will, for You are my God.

PSALM 143:10

BIBLE READING: PSALM 143:7–9

AUGUST

-29-

God is the one who gives the commands; we are the ones who obey. He never has to explain Himself; He never has to ask permission. Nor does He predict ahead of time that we're just about to encounter a closed door. He is shaping us into the image of His Son, regardless of the pain and heartache that may require. Those lessons are learned a little easier when we remember that we are not in charge, He is.

Christ also suffered for you,
leaving you an example . . . to follow.

1 PETER 2:21

BIBLE READING: 1 PETER 5:1—6

CHARLES SWINDOLL

AUGUST

-30-

If you're getting ready to go off to school or getting ready to launch a new phase of your career, don't do it without first establishing a regular time to meet alone with the Lord. . . . Your spiritual future depends on it. Without that commitment to saturate your life with God's Word, you step into the unknown future at your own risk.

In your faith, supply moral excellence,
and in your moral excellence, knowledge.

2 PETER 1:5

BIBLE READING: 2 PETER 1:1—15

AUGUST

-31-

To be our great High Priest, Christ had to be unique. He had to represent both God and man. He had to be the God-Man—undiminished deity and genuine humanity in one person. That's a wonderful truth. When you go to your Savior in prayer, laying your petitions before Him, you go to the One whose heart beats with yours, because He has known pain and discomfort, He has been reproached and offended. He has been hated and ignored and rejected.

Consider Jesus, the . . . High Priest of our confession.

HEBREWS 3:1

BIBLE READING: HEBREWS 2:10—3:11

CHARLES SWINDOLL

SEPTEMBER

ACCEPTANCE IS RESTING
IN GOD'S GOODNESS.

SEPTEMBER

-1-

The word "hurry" shows up far more in our vocabulary than it does in God's plan. Waiting goes against human nature. We like to hurry, and so we want God to hurry, too. But He doesn't. God prepares us during times when the whole world seems to be going on without us. He patiently, deliberately, steadily, molds us in the shadows, so we might be prepared for later years when He chooses to use us in the spotlight.

Rest in the LORD and wait patiently for Him.

PSALM 37:7

BIBLE READING: PSALM 130

CHARLES SWINDOLL

SEPTEMBER

-2-

In a strange way, an elevator is a microcosm of our world today: a crowded impersonal place where anonymity, isolation, and independence are the norm.

How do we come to terms with this? Our Savior modeled the answer perfectly. He listened. He served. He touched as well as stayed in touch. He walked with people . . . never took the elevator. The only escape from indifference is to think of people as our most cherished recourse.

When Jesus . . . saw her weeping . . . He was deeply moved.

JOHN 11:33

BIBLE READING: JOHN 11:1–44

SEPTEMBER

-3-

The church is a place for young and old, single and married, truck driver or brain surgeon, saint or seeker, you name it.

Whether we are normal or nearly normal or hoping someday to be normal, we belong. Whatever our situation, we are all looking for the magnificent truths of God, for genuine Christian fellowship and togetherness. In the body of Christ we are all the same: forgiven, but not perfect. Except for One.

Preserve the unity of the Spirit in the bond of peace.

EPHESIANS 4:3

BIBLE READING: EPHESIANS 4:1–7

CHARLES SWINDOLL

SEPTEMBER

-4-

Contrary to popular opinion, work is not the result of the curse. Adam was given the task of cultivating and keeping the Garden before sin ever entered (Gen. 2:15). Then what was the curse? It was the addition of "thorns and thistles" that turned work into a "toil."

Today, it isn't literal briars and stinging nettles that give us fits: it's thorny people whose thistlelike attitudes add just enough irritation to make the job . . . well, a *job*. The difference is people. The place you work will never be better than you make it.

He who walks in integrity walks securely.

PROVERBS 10:9

BIBLE READING: PROVERBS 10

SEPTEMBER

-5-

At a time when many people in his place would be looking back in regret, wondering what life would have been like in a different profession, Paul repudiates the past and looks with confidence to the future. His strong determination kept him focused on the ultimate goal—pleasing Christ all the way to the goal, even in chains. It's the picture of a runner running for the tape at the end of the race, straining forward in strong determination. Paul said, "I'm not looking back. I'm stretching for the prize."

I press on toward the goal for the prize
of the upward call of God in Christ Jesus.

PHILIPPIANS 3:14

BIBLE READING: PHILIPPIANS 2:12—18

CHARLES SWINDOLL

SEPTEMBER

-6-

What we want to *do* is not nearly as important as what we want to *be*. Doing is usually concerned with a vocation or career, *how we make a living.* Being is much deeper. It relates to character, who we are, and *how we make a life.* Doing is tied with accomplishments and tangible things—like salary and trophies. Being, on the other hand, has more to do with intangibles, much of which can't be measured by objective yardsticks and impressive awards.

Man looks at the outward
appearance, but the LORD looks at the heart.

1 SAMUEL 16:7

BIBLE READING: ECCLESIASTES 2:11; 1 SAMUEL 16:1–13

SEPTEMBER

-7-

Jesus encouraged tolerance. Be tolerant of those who don't look like you, who don't dress like you, who don't care about the things you care about, who don't vote like you. Furthermore, be tolerant of those whose fine points of theology differ from yours, whose worship style is different. Be tolerant of young if you are older . . . and be tolerant of the aging if you are young.

Jesus wanted His followers to be people of simple faith, modeled in grace, based on truth.

The fruit of the Spirit is love, joy, peace, patience, kindness.

GALATIANS 5:22

BIBLE READING: MATTHEW 7:1–6

CHARLES SWINDOLL

SEPTEMBER

-8-

Wisdom comes privately from God as a by-product of right decisions, godly reactions, and the application of scriptural principles to daily circumstances. Wisdom comes, for example, not from seeking after a ministry . . . but more from anticipating the fruit of a disciplined life. Not from trying to do great things for God . . . but more from being faithful to the small, obscure tasks few people ever see.

With Him are wisdom and might;
to Him belong counsel and understanding.

JOB 12:13

BIBLE READING: JOB 12:13–25

SEPTEMBER

-9-

God saw Jesus as our substitute. God also saw His Son's suffering as a part of His sovereign will. The Savior's suffering, therefore, pleased Him. Yet the Father was not unconcerned about His Son when He went to Calvary. The people of Jesus' day may have dismissed Him as insignificant, but certainly not the Father! It pleased the Father because He wanted to show us mercy.

The LORD was pleased to crush Him, putting Him to grief.

ISAIAH 53:10

BIBLE READING: 1 PETER 2:21–24

CHARLES SWINDOLL

SEPTEMBER
-10-

There is an old Greek motto that says: *You will break the bow if you keep it always bent.*

Which, being loosely translated, means, "There's more to life than hard work." Loosening the strings on our bow means when we have some leisure, we live it up. We deliberately erase from our minds that we are a cop or a nurse or a lawyer or a preacher. We do stuff that helps us stay sane. And fun to be with.

Whatever you do in word or deed, do all in the name of the Lord Jesus, giving thanks through Him to God the Father.

COLOSSIANS 3:17

BIBLE READING: 1 CHRONICLES 15:25–29; 29:6–28

SEPTEMBER

-11-

Every dawn, before you awaken, life makes a delivery to your front door, rings the doorbell, and runs. Each package is cleverly wrapped. It comprises a series of challenging opportunities brilliantly disguised as unsolved problems.

When you hear the bell ring in the morning, try something new. Have Christ answer the door.

I will never desert you, nor will I ever forsake you.

HEBREWS 13:5

BIBLE READING: LUKE 12:22–34; COLOSSIANS 4:5

CHARLES SWINDOLL

SEPTEMBER
-12-

Men and women are different, and these differences don't decrease or disappear once people get married.

Harmonious partnerships are the result of hard work; they never "just happen." I don't know of anything that helps this process more than deep, honest, regular communication. Read those last four words again, please. That's not just talking; it's also listening. And not just listening, but also hearing. Not just hearing, but also responding calmly and kindly. In private. With mutual respect.

Be kind to one another, tender-hearted, forgiving each other.

EPHESIANS 4:32

BIBLE READING: EPHESIANS 5:22–33

SEPTEMBER
-13-

The suffering you endure can ultimately turn to your benefit. God is working. Only He knows the end from the beginning, and He knows you and your needs far better than even you do. Don't ask, "Why is this happening to me?" Rather, ask the question, "How should I respond?" Otherwise, you'll miss the beneficial role suffering plays in life.

I can do all things through Him who strengthens me.

PHILIPPIANS 4:13

BIBLE READING: HEBREWS 12:1–3

CHARLES SWINDOLL

SEPTEMBER
-14-

Your humiliations, your struggles, your battles, your weaknesses, your feelings of inadequacy, your helplessness, even your so-called "disqualifying" infirmities are precisely what *make* you effective. I would go further and say they represent the stuff of greatness. Once you are convinced of your own weakness and no longer try to hide it, you embrace the power of Christ.

Not that we are adequate in ourselves to consider anything as coming from ourselves, but our adequacy is from God.

2 CORINTHIANS 3:5

BIBLE READING: PSALM 77; 2 CORINTHIANS 3:1–6

SEPTEMBER

-15-

There is no instant route to roots. Nor is it a high-profile process.

Mark it down—there won't be a seminar next week that promises "Strong roots in five days or your money back." The process is slow. The process is silent. But in the long run the final product will be irreplaceable . . . invaluable.

Walk in [Christ] . . . having been
firmly rooted and . . . built up in Him.

COLOSSIANS 2:6−7

BIBLE READING: EPHESIANS 3:1−21; COLOSSIANS 2:1−23

CHARLES SWINDOLL

SEPTEMBER

-16-

Spiritually speaking, the ultimate goal or purpose of our lives is "His good pleasure." Our lives are to be lived for God's greater glory—not our own selfish desires.

Are we left to do so all alone? Is it our task to gut it out, grit our teeth, and do His will? Not at all. Here's the balance: *God is at work in us!* He is the one who gives us strength and empowers our diligence. As He pours into us, we do the things that bring Him pleasure.

It is God who is as work in you,
both to will and to work for His good pleasure.

PHILIPPIANS 2:13

BIBLE READING: PHILIPPIANS 2:1—18

SEPTEMBER

-17-

Deep within the recesses of our minds there is this invisible, albeit hostile, battleground. On one side are my fleshly desires; on the other, the blessed Spirit of God. One is dark; the other light. One is evil; the other righteous.

The good news is: We don't have to serve the old master any longer! Now that we have our Lord's divine, dynamic presence perpetually living within us, we can live above all that . . . on a consistent basis!

We naturally love to do evil things that are just the opposite from the things that the Holy Spirit tells us to do.

GALATIANS 5:17, TLB

BIBLE READING: GALATIANS 5:16—25

CHARLES SWINDOLL

SEPTEMBER

-18-

If you wish to be a man or woman of God who desires to live a godly life that will leave its mark upon this world, you must stand in the shadow of your Savior. Trust Him to work through the trials you encounter, through the extreme circumstances you cannot handle on your own. He is still the God of impossible situations. He does what no earthly individual can do.

Trust in the LORD and do good. . . . Cultivate faithfulness.

PSALM 37:3

BIBLE READING: ROMANS 9:31–39

SEPTEMBER

-19-

It's amazing how you can get carried away from worries and woes and self-concern when you start naming out loud what you're thankful for. Right away your focus shifts from your needs to the Father's graciousness and love.

Try it!

*Enter His gates with thanksgiving
and His courts with praise.*

PSALM 100:4

BIBLE READING: PSALM 101

SEPTEMBER

-20-

A number of years ago, somebody counted the promises in the Bible and totaled up 7,474. I can't verify that number, but I do know that there are thousands of promises that grab the reader and say, "Believe me! Accept me! Hold on to me!" And of all the promises in the Bible, the ones that often mean the most are the promises that offer hope at the end of affliction. Those promises that tell us, "It's worth it. Walk with Me. Trust Me. I will reward you."

Who is wise? Let him give
heed to . . . the lovingkindnesses of the LORD.

PSALM 107:43

BIBLE READING: PSALM 119: 97–104

SEPTEMBER
-21-

God has not designed us to live like hermits in a cave. He has designed us to live in friendship and fellowship and community with others. That's why the church, the body of Christ, is so very important, for it is there that we are drawn together in love and mutual encouragement. We're meant to be a part of one another's lives.

Walk in love, just as Christ also
loved you and gave Himself up for us.

EPHESIANS 5:2

BIBLE READING: EPHESIANS 5:1–10

SEPTEMBER

-22-

Jesus took the twelve disciples across a lake to enjoy some R & R alone on a mountainside. Who knows what they did for fun? Maybe they swam or sat around a campfire and told a few jokes. Whatever, you can count on this—they laughed. Today, Cynthia and I prefer to hop on an old Harley. If Jesus lived on earth today, He might ride with us. But something in me says He probably wouldn't get a tattoo. Then again, who knows? He did a lot of stuff that made the legalists squirm.

We overwhelmingly conquer through Him who loved us.

ROMANS 8:37

BIBLE READING: ROMANS 8:26–34

SEPTEMBER

-23-

I don't know why a tornado destroys one neighborhood and not another. I just know that even in this calamity God's plan is not frustrated or altered. Either that, or He isn't God. He is not sitting on the edge of heaven, wondering what will happen next. That's not the God of the Scriptures.

Remember, nothing is a surprise to God.

I hope in You, O LORD; You will answer, O LORD my God.

PSALM 38:15

BIBLE READING: PSALM 38:9—22

CHARLES SWINDOLL

SEPTEMBER

-24-

When you wait on the Lord, you don't have to go out on a hillside, eat birdseed, and strum a guitar. You don't have to wear a robe and live in a hut in Tibet for the winter. You need to sit down quietly, by yourself, alone with the Lord. You think His thoughts, You recall words from His Book. You feed your soul with His manna.

To You I lift up my eyes,
O You who are enthroned in the heavens!

PSALM 123:1

BIBLE READING: PSALM 123

SEPTEMBER

-25-

Living out your faith at the office or in that university dorm or in your high school may feel pretty lonely. Walking by faith and honoring the Lord in your profession may seem futile at times. In fact, in your own lifetime, you may never know the significance of your walk of faith. But God will use you in His special plan for your life, just as He has countless others through the centuries.

His mercy is upon generation
after generation toward those who fear Him.

LUKE 1:50

BIBLE READING; PSALM 19:8; 25:8; 18:30

CHARLES SWINDOLL

SEPTEMBER
-26-

Can you make these four statements? If you can
. . . *will* you?

1. I am here by God's appointment.
2. I am in His keeping.
3. I am under His training.
4. He will show me His purposes in His time.

By God's appointment, in God's keeping, under
His training, for His time. What an outstanding
summary of what it means to trust in the Lord with
all your heart!

I know You can do all things,
and that no purpose of Yours can be thwarted.

JOB 42:2

BIBLE READING: JOB 42

SEPTEMBER
-27-

Sometimes we step into a situation that is clearly the will of God for us. We have reflected on it, we have gotten counsel from people we respect, and we have peace about it . . . and we're not in two weeks before we realize, *This is a can of worms!* This is work! So even within the will of God, there are surprises and struggles. But we still have peace, knowing that we are the one who is supposed to deal with this can of worms.

Consider it all joy . . . when you encounter various trials knowing that the testing of your faith produces endurance.

JAMES 1:2—3

BIBLE READING: 2 TIMOTHY 3:12; 1 PETER 4:1—2

CHARLES SWINDOLL

SEPTEMBER

-28-

Don't get stuck on where you *were*. Don't waste your time focusing on *what you used to be*. Remember, the hope we have in Christ means there's a brighter tomorrow. The sins are forgiven. The shame is canceled out. We're no longer chained to a deep, dark pit of the past. Grace gives us wings to soar.

You are a God of forgiveness, gracious and compassionate.

NEHEMIAH 9:17

BIBLE READING: PHILIPPIANS 3:12—21

SEPTEMBER

-29-

When people are suffering, they turn to those they know will understand—those who have been there themselves. That is why it is so important that we understand the suffering of Jesus and His death on the cross. Because He was fully human, as well as fully God, He understands God's demanding penalty for sin, just as He understands the pain of our infirmities. He knows exactly what we are thinking and feeling.

We do not have a high priest who cannot sympathize with our weaknesses, but One who has been tempted in all things as we are, yet without sin.

HEBREWS 4:15

BIBLE READING: HEBREWS 2:14–18; 4:14–16

CHARLES SWINDOLL

SEPTEMBER

-30-

We admire Paul for his strength in trials. We want to applaud his fierce determination against vicious persecution. If the man were alive today, he would not tolerate our congratulations. "No, no, no. You don't understand. *I'm not strong. The One who pours his power into me is strong. My strength comes from my weakness.*"

It is that kind of response that brings divine strength and allows it to spring into action.

"By the grace of God I am what I am."

1 CORINTHIANS 15:10

BIBLE READING: 1 CORINTHIANS 15:1–11;
EPHESIANS 3:14–21

OCTOBER

JOY IS A CHOICE.

OCTOBER

-1-

In choosing those who would represent Christ and establish His church, God picked some of the most unusual individuals imaginable: unschooled fishermen, a tax collector (!), a mystic, a doubter, and a former Pharisee who had persecuted Christians. He continued to pick some very unusual persons down through the ages. In fact, He seems to delight in such surprising choices to this very day.

Breaking molds is His specialty.

The Son of Man has come
to seek and to save that which was lost.

LUKE 19:10

BIBLE READING: LUKE 19:1—10

CHARLES SWINDOLL

OCTOBER

-2-

Fathomless truths *about* God and profound insights *from* God produce within us a wisdom that enables us to think *with* God. Such wisdom comes from His Spirit who, alone, can plumb the depths and reveal His mind.

The hurried, the greedy, the impatient cannot enter into such mysteries. God grants such understanding only to those who wait in silence. It takes time. It calls for solitude.

We speak God's wisdom in a mystery, the hidden wisdom.

1 CORINTHIANS 2:7

BIBLE READING: 1 CORINTHIANS 2:7–13

OCTOBER

-3-

The Bible exhorts all believers to be ready to "make a defense" for our faith. The Greek word for "defense" is *apologia*. It carries the idea of setting forth evidence.

If a friend happened to be struggling to find the truth, or a coworker challenged your belief system, could you deliver enough evidence to provide a compelling defense? It's part of being a calming witness in a world spinning wildly off center.

Always [be] ready to make a defense to everyone
who asks you to give an account for the hope that is in you.

1 PETER 3:15

BIBLE READING: 1 PETER 3:13—22

OCTOBER

-4-

Why try to be like anybody else?

Cultivate your own capabilities. Your own style. Appreciate the members of your family or your fellowship for who they are, even though their outlook or style may be miles different from yours. Rabbits don't fly. Eagles don't swim. Ducks look funny trying to climb. Squirrels don't have feathers.

Stop comparing. Enjoy being you!

How precious are Your thoughts to me, O God!

PSALM 139:17

BIBLE READING: ISAIAH 40:25–26; 46:5–9

OCTOBER

-5-

Adversity or prosperity, both are tough tests on our balance. To stay balanced throughout adversity, resiliency is required. But to stay balanced through prosperity—ah, that demands *integrity*. The swift wind of compromise is a lot more devastating than the sudden jolt of misfortune.

That's why walking on a wire is harder than standing up in a storm. Height has a strange way of disturbing our balance.

A good name is to be more desired than great wealth.

PROVERBS 22:1

BIBLE READING: DANIEL 1:1—21

CHARLES SWINDOLL

OCTOBER

-6-

The word "word" remains the most powerful of all four-letter words. Colors fade. Shorelines erode. Temples crumble. Empires fall. But "a word fitly spoken" endures. Fitly spoken words are *right* words . . . the precise words needed for the occasion.

Mark Twain, a unique wordsmith himself, once wrote: "The difference between the right word and almost the right word is the difference between lightning and a lightning bug." And what power those " right words" contain!

A word fitly spoken is like apples of gold in settings of silver.

PROVERBS 25:11, NKJV

BIBLE READING: PROVERBS 15:7; 16:24

OCTOBER

-7-

When it comes to His own portrait, Christ paints it under the shadow of the cross, with the browns and grays and blacks of realism. No frame. No fame. No spotlight. It's the truth on display. It's the Man of Sorrows, who was acquainted with grief—the One who was pierced through for our transgressions and crushed for our iniquities.

We give Him our highest praise as we sing, "Worthy is the Lamb that was slain."

Worthy is the Lamb that was slain
to receive power and riches and wisdom and might.

REVELATION 5:12

BIBLE READING: REVELATION 5

OCTOBER

-8-

THERE'S NO NEED TO TAKE GOD SERIOUSLY.

I know of no philosophy more popular today. It's the reason so many folks are caught in the do-your-own-thing *sin*drome.

If you don't take God seriously, there's no need to take your marriage seriously . . . or the rearing of children . . . or such character traits as submission, faithfulness, sexual purity, humility, repentance, and honesty.

To whom shall I speak and give warning that they may hear?

JEREMIAH 6:10

BIBLE READING: JEREMIAH 6:9–21

OCTOBER

-9-

I am concerned that we slow down and quiet down and gear down our lives so that intermittently each week we carve out time for quietness, solitude, thought, prayer, meditation, and soul searching. Oh, how much agitation will begin to fade away . . . how insignificant petty differences will seem . . . how big God will become and how small our troubles will appear!

Be still, and know that I am God.

PSALM 46:10, NKJV

BIBLE READING: ISAIAH 30:15–18; MARK 6:30–32

CHARLES SWINDOLL

OCTOBER

-10-

With Moses it was murder. With Elijah it was deep depression. With Peter it was public denial. With Samson it was recurring lust. With Thomas it was cynical doubting. With Jacob it was deception.

Some of the greatest saints have crawled out of the deepest, dirtiest, most scandalous "holes" you could imagine. And it was that which kept them humble, honest men and women of God, unwilling to be glorified or idolized.

The LORD God helps Me, therefore, I am not disgraced.

ISAIAH 50:7

BIBLE READING: ISAIAH 50

OCTOBER

-11-

The late Leonard Bernstein, composer and famed conductor, was asked what he believed to be the most difficult instrument in the orchestra to play. He responded, "Second fiddle!"

When you examine the life of any great individual, you soon discover an entire section of second-fiddlers, super people, gifted in their own rights, but content to play their parts seated in the second chair.

The way of the LORD is a stronghold to the upright.

PROVERBS 10:29

BIBLE READING: LUKE 6:20—29

OCTOBER

-12-

It isn't easy to trust God in times of adversity. Feelings of distress, despair, and darkness trouble our souls as we wonder if God truly cares about our plight. But *not to trust* Him is to doubt His sovereignty and to question His goodness. In order to trust God we must view our adverse circumstances through eyes of faith, not our senses.

Do not fear, for I am with you;
do not anxiously look about you, for I am your God.

ISAIAH 41:10

BIBLE READING: PSALM 108; 1 CHRONICLES 29:11–12

OCTOBER

-13-

"What is that to you?" asks Christ. When it comes to this matter of doing His will, God has not said that you must answer for anyone else except yourself. Quit looking around for equality! Stop concerning yourself with the need of others to do what you are doing. Or endure what you have been called to endure. God chooses the roles we play. Each part is unique.

"If I want him to remain
until I come, what is that to you? You follow Me!"

JOHN 21:22

BIBLE READING: MARK 1:14–20; 10:21–31

CHARLES SWINDOLL

OCTOBER

-14-

About the time we are tempted to think we can handle things all alone—boom! We run into some obstacle and need assistance. We discover all over again that we are not nearly as self-sufficient as we thought.

In spite of our high-tech world and efficient procedures, people remain the essential ingredient of life. When we forget that, a strange thing happens: We start treating people like inconveniences instead of assets.

Let the word of Christ richly
dwell within you . . . teaching . . . one another.

COLOSSIANS 3:16

BIBLE READING: COLOSSIANS 3:12–17

OCTOBER

-15-

We do not belong to ourselves, nor should we operate independently of the Spirit of God. Now that we have been converted, we are the Lord's, and as our Master, He has every right to use us in whatever way He chooses. We have one major objective: to "glorify God in [our] body."

Since the believer's body is considered the "temple of the Holy Spirit," it stands to reason that He should be glorified in it and through it. He owns it!

For you have been bought
with a price, therefore glorify God in your body.

1 CORINTHIANS 6:19—20

BIBLE READING: 1 CORINTHIANS 6:12—20

CHARLES SWINDOLL

OCTOBER

-16-

Remind yourself of God's promises regarding generosity. God promises if you sow bountifully, you will reap bountifully. So give! Give abundantly! Even extravagant giving is honored by God. I've never known anyone who went bad because he or she was too generous. Remind yourself of His promises regarding generosity and start giving!

He who sows bountifully will also reap bountifully.

2 CORINTHIANS 9:6

BIBLE READING: 2 CORINTHIANS 9:1–11

OCTOBER

-17-

The most significant decision I can make on a day-to-day basis is my choice of attitude. It is more important than my past, my education, my bankroll, my successes or failures, fame or pain, what other people think of me or say about me, my circumstances, or my position. When my attitudes are right, there's no barrier too high, no valley too deep, no dream too extreme, no challenge too great.

Be imitators of God as beloved children.

EPHESIANS 5:1

BIBLE READING: 2 THESSALONIANS 2:16–17

CHARLES SWINDOLL

OCTOBER

-18-

God knows where we are. Sometimes we forget this. Sometimes we even feel that God has forgotten us. He hasn't. God knows exactly where we are. So when you are afflicted with those forsaken feelings, when you're on the verge of throwing a pity party, go back to the Word of God. God says, "I know where you are."

I will hold you by the hand and watch over you.

ISAIAH 42:6

BIBLE READING: PSALM 20

OCTOBER

-19-

It takes God to make the heart right. When I have a wrong attitude, I look at life humanly. When I have a right attitude, I look at life divinely.

The fear of the LORD is the beginning of wisdom,
and the knowledge of the Holy One is understanding.

PROVERBS 9:10

BIBLE READING: PROVERBS 9:1–12

CHARLES SWINDOLL

OCTOBER

-20-

If we were declared 99.9 percent righteous, some verses would have to be rewritten. Like Isaiah 1:18, which might then read: "'Come now, and let us reason together,' says the Lord, 'though your sins are as scarlet, they will be light pink.'"

Nonsense! The promise of sins forgiven is all or nothing.

Though your sins are
like scarlet, they shall be as white as snow.

ISAIAH 1:18

BIBLE READING: PSALM 130

OCTOBER

-21-

Did you know that laughter actually works like a medicine in our systems? It exercises our lungs and stimulates our circulation. It takes our minds off our troubles and massages our emotions. Laughter decreases tension. When we laugh, a sort of temporary anesthesia is released within us that blocks the pain as our attention is diverted.

Laughter is one of the healthiest exercises we can enjoy. It literally brings healing.

A joyful heart is good medicine,
but a broken spirit dries up the bones.

PROVERBS 17:22

BIBLE READING: PSALM 35:9; 100:1; 1 PETER 4:13

CHARLES SWINDOLL

OCTOBER

-22-

God is the Potter; we are the clay. He's the Shepherd; we are the sheep. He's the Master; we are the servants. No matter how educated we are, no matter how much power and influence we may think we have, none of that qualifies us to grasp the first particle of why He does what He does when He does it and how He chooses to do it.

My thoughts are not your thoughts,
nor are your ways My ways.

ISAIAH 55:8

BIBLE READING: JOHN 10:1–18

OCTOBER

-23-

The workings of God are not related to our clocks; they are related to our crises. That's why God doesn't care if this is the last day you can buy that car on sale. It doesn't bother God that it is the first day of summer or high noon or a quarter after seven or ten minutes to one in the morning. His timing is unrelated to Planet Earth's clock time. So while waiting, look beyond the present. And the best way to do that is to pray! Prayer gives a calming perspective.

The effective prayer of a
righteous man can accomplish much.

JAMES 5:16

BIBLE READING: JAMES 1:1–8; 5:13–18

CHARLES SWINDOLL

OCTOBER

-24-

I have a book in my hand. If I were to hand it to you and say, "It's yours; I'd like you to have it," and you were to take it, I would be giving you a gift. When you take the gift, you become the possessor of the gift. It's yours.

Salvation is a gift. God reached out to you and me at the cross, where His Son paid the penalty of sin by dying in our place. All He asks is that we reach out in faith and take it.

By grace you have been saved through faith;
and that not of yourselves, it is the gift of God.

EPHESIANS 2:8

BIBLE READING: EPHESIANS 1:1—14

OCTOBER

-25-

Nothing is more encouraging than knowing for sure that we are in the will of God. Then, no matter what happens, we can stand fast.

We can be out of a job but know that we are in the will of God. We can face a threatening situation but know that we are in the will of God. We can have the odds stacked against us but know that we are in the will of God. Nothing intimidates those who know they are in the will of God.

That you may be filled with the knowledge of His will.

COLOSSIANS 1:9

BIBLE READING: COLOSSIANS 1:1–12

CHARLES SWINDOLL

OCTOBER

-26-

Mercy is the active compassion God demonstrates to the miserable. When we are in a time of deep distress, and God activates His compassion to bring about relief, we've experienced mercy.

Mercy. It isn't passive pity. It isn't simply understanding. It isn't mere sorrow. It's a divine action on our behalf through which God brings about a sense of relief.

As we have received mercy, we do not lost heart.

2 CORINTHIANS 4:1

BIBLE READING: 2 CORINTHIANS 4:1—12

OCTOBER

-27-

Are you a wife and homemaker who feels that your contribution to God's service is not noteworthy? Do you see other people as *special* or *called* or *talented*?

You may be in the very midst of a ministry and not even realize it. (What greater ministry can there be, for example, than that of a faithful and loving wife and mother?) Your ministry may be to just two or three people and that's all. No matter what role you fill in life, you're not unimportant when it comes to standing alone for truth.

Through love serve one another.

GALATIANS 5:13

BIBLE READING: GALATIANS 5:13–26

CHARLES SWINDOLL

OCTOBER

-28-

God's sense of humor has intrigued me for years. What amazes me, however, is the number of people who don't think He has one. For the life of me, I can't figure out why they can't see it. He made you and me, didn't He? And what about all those funny-looking creatures that keep drawing us back to the zoo? If they aren't proof of our Creator's sense of humor, I don't know what is. Have you taken a close look at a wombat or a two-toed sloth lately?

By Him all things were created,
both in the heavens and on earth.

COLOSSIANS 1:16

BIBLE READING: GENESIS 1

OCTOBER

-29-

When I am treated unfairly, God's mercy relieves my bitterness. When I have been in a dungeon of unfair treatment, bitterness becomes my enemy, but mercy relieves it.

When I grieve over loss, God's mercy relieves my sorrow. Not instantly, but ultimately.

You have seen my affliction;
You have known the troubles of my soul.

PSALM 31:7

BIBLE READING: PSALM 31:1—8

CHARLES SWINDOLL

OCTOBER

-30-

The beautiful music of living is composed, practiced, and perfected in the harmony of home. The freedom to laugh long and loudly . . . the encouragement to participate in memories and deepen our roots in the rich, rare soil of authentic happiness. These are part of the things God gives us to enjoy.

God . . . richly supplies us with all things to enjoy.

1 TIMOTHY 6:17

BIBLE READING: ROMANS 8:32; PSALM 145:3–7

OCTOBER

-31-

People who know who they are, who possess a clear sense of their mission, and who understand God's plan and purpose for their lives, are people who experience genuine fulfillment. That doesn't mean they don't face extreme obstacles. Rather, it means they have learned to face those challenges in ways that transform obstacles into opportunities. Rather than stumbling over them, they press on *through* them.

The way of the LORD is a stronghold to
the upright. . . . The righteous will never be shaken.

PROVERBS 10:29—30

BIBLE READING: JAMES 1:12—18

CHARLES SWINDOLL

NOVEMBER

THANKFUL LIVING IS

THANKS GIVING.

NOVEMBER

-1-

G od would love to piece together the shattered fragments of your life. But He is waiting . . . graciously waiting until you are tired of the life you are living . . . until you see it for what it really is.

Until you are weary of coping . . . of taking charge of your own life . . . until you realize the mess you are making of it.

Until you recognize your need for Him. He's waiting . . .

The LORD longs to be gracious to you,
and therefore He waits on high to have compassion on you.

ISAIAH 30:18

BIBLE READING: MATTHEW 11:28–30; REVELATION 3:20

NOVEMBER

-2-

Redeemed from a life of vicious brutality as a legalistic Pharisee, Paul turned the corner, repented, and through Christ's empowering became a gentle soul, gracious and affirming. Understanding. Forgiving. Approachable. He reached the place where he was willing not only to offer hope to the Gentiles, but to live among them, though he himself would bleed pure Jewish blood. No one that I know endured the level of hardship he did as a good soldier of Christ.

Be strong in the grace that is
in Christ Jesus . . . as a good soldier of Christ Jesus.

2 TIMOTHY 2:1, 3

BIBLE READING: 2 TIMOTHY 2:1—13

NOVEMBER

-3-

L ife is full of journeys. Some are dull excursions we grudgingly take out of sheer duty. Others are thrilling adventures we embark on with eyes of faith. But changes await you . . . changes in you.

No journey is more life changing than your inner spiritual journey back to the Cross. In all your travels, have you gone there? If not, are you willing to take that first step? It's a journey you will never regret, I can assure you, and one you will never forget.

I shall walk before the LORD.

PSALM 116:9

BIBLE READING: PSALM 116:1–11

CHARLES SWINDOLL

NOVEMBER

-4-

There is no greater deception than *self*-deception. It is a tragic trap laid for everyone, but especially vulnerable are those who have achieved . . . and start reading their own clippings.

Here's my advice:

1. Get a good education—*but get over it.*
2. Reach the maximum of your potential—but *don't talk about it.*
3. Walk devotedly with God—but *don't try to look like it.*

*If anyone thinks he is something
when he is nothing, he deceives himself.*

GALATIANS 6:3

BIBLE READING: LUKE 18:9–14; JOHN 12:42–43

NOVEMBER

-5-

G od knows what He's about. If He has you
sidelined, out of the action for awhile, He
knows what He's doing. You just stay faithful . . .
stay flexible . . . stay available. Learn your lessons
well in the schoolroom of obscurity. At the precise
moment He will reach for you and launch you to
His place of appointment.

I will not fail you or forsake you.

JOSHUA 1:5—6

BIBLE READING: JOSHUA 1:1—6

CHARLES SWINDOLL

NOVEMBER

-6-

When God is in charge, both the timing and the extent of whatever success He may have in mind for you will be surprising. This does not mean there is no place for planning or goal-setting or diligence; it just means we refuse to make success our private shrine. When God is in it, we're surprised at it rather than smug about it.

Instead of spending all those hours pushing and promoting, you'll wind up with more time for friends and family and the Lord.

Seek first His kingdom and His righteousness.

MATTHEW 6:33

BIBLE READING: MATTHEW 6:24–34

NOVEMBER

-7-

Today the cross is an object of veneration. Designed into exquisite jewelry and artistic statuary, the cross has become a thing of beauty.

People of the first century would be shocked to see our modern treatment of what was, to them, an object of brutality. It meant the most hideous, anguished death imaginable.

The ends of the earth will remember and
turn to the LORD, and . . . will worship before You.

PSALM 22:27

BIBLE READING: JOB 37:22; 2 PETER 1:16; GALATIANS 6:14

CHARLES SWINDOLL

NOVEMBER

-8-

Jesus "learned obedience from the things which He suffered," not *in spite of* those things.

Do you have a problem? You're smiling back at me. "*A* problem? Would you believe *several dozen* problems?" If you listen to the voices around you, you'll search for a substitute—an escape route. You'll miss the fact that each of those problems is a God-appointed instructor ready to stretch you and challenge you and deepen your walk with Him. Growth and wisdom await you!

He learned obedience from the things which He suffered.

HEBREWS 5:8

BIBLE READING: 1 PETER 4:12–19; JAMES 1:1–12

NOVEMBER

-9-

The Bible is running over with promises and encouragement directly related to the return of our Lord Jesus Christ. In the New Testament alone the events related to Christ's coming are mentioned over 300 times.

Critics have denied it. Cynics have laughed at it. Scholars have ignored it. The return of our Savior will continue to be attacked and misused and denied. But there it stands, solid as a stone, offering us hope and encouragement amidst despair and unbelief.

Looking for the blessed hope and
the appearing . . . of our . . . Savior, Christ Jesus.

TITUS 2:13

BIBLE READING: JAMES 5:7–8; ACTS 1:1–11

CHARLES SWINDOLL

NOVEMBER
-10-

Though change is good, it's rarely easy or pleasant. We're most interested in pursuing the comfortable route. We prefer the road more frequently traveled. Everything within us scrambles to stay on trails already blazed. But God often leads us down unknown paths filled with narrow passages and surprising turns.

He Himself knows our frame;
He is mindful that we are but dust.

PSALM 103:14

BIBLE READING: PSALM 111:1—6

NOVEMBER

-11-

Life is filled with God-appointed storms. But two things should comfort us. First, these squalls surge across *everyone's* horizon. Second, we all *need* them. God has no other method more effective. The massive blows and shattering blasts (not to mention the little, constant irritations) smooth us, humble us, and compel us to submit to *His* script and *His* chosen role for our lives.

The LORD is great in power,
. . . in whirlwind and storm is His way.

NAHUM 1:3

BIBLE READING: DEUTERONOMY 4:27–31; DANIEL 4:28–37

CHARLES SWINDOLL

NOVEMBER
-12-

You need me. I need you. Both of us need a few kindred spirits, people who understand us and encourage us. Both of us need friends who are willing to risk to help us, and, yes, at times, to rescue us. Friends like that make life more fun. But all of us—you, me, *all of us*—need a Savior. The everlasting relief He brings is enough to make us not only laugh again, but laugh forever.

In Your presence is fullness of joy.

PSALM 16:11

BIBLE READING: PSALM 25:12–15

NOVEMBER

-13-

God's wisdom is not discovered from human sources. The human mind, all of its own, cannot plumb the depths of God's truths. Those truths must come from the Godhead. And the One appointed to that specific task? The Holy Spirit, who lives within every child of God. He resides within us, not to be dormant and passive, but actively engaged in revealing God's hidden wisdom.

When He, the Spirit of truth,
comes, He will guide you into all the truth.

JOHN 16:13

BIBLE READING: 1 CORINTHIANS 2:6–9

CHARLES SWINDOLL

NOVEMBER

-14-

God reached into your life when you were merely a tiny embryo and began to shape you within. He originated you. He began to put you together while you were still in the soft silence of your mother's womb.

Mother Nature didn't make you. Fate did not shape you, neither were you just a biological combination of mother and dad in a moment of sexual passion. God (and no other), made you!

You wove me in my mother's womb. I will
give thanks to You, for I am fearfully and wonderfully made.

PSALM 139:13–14

BIBLE READING: PSALM 139:1–16

NOVEMBER

-15-

Great wealth is not related to money. It is an attitude of satisfaction ("enough is enough") coupled with inner peace (an absence of churning) plus a day-by-day, moment-by-moment walk with God. . . .

In a word, the secret is *contentment*.

Whatever things were gain to me,
those things I have counted as loss for the sake of Christ.

PHILIPPIANS 3:7

BIBLE READING: PHILIPPIANS 4:12–14; 2:1–13

NOVEMBER

-16-

The key phrase in the verse below is "when He has tried me." You see, there is no hurry-up process for finding and shaping gold. The process of discovering, processing, purifying, and shaping gold is a lengthy, painstaking process. Affliction is gold in the making for the child of God, and God is the one who determines how long the process take. He alone is the Refiner.

He knows the way I take;
when He has tried me, I shall come forth as gold.

JOB 23:10

BIBLE READING: COLOSSIANS 2:1–7

NOVEMBER

-17-

There's a sense of stability in trusting the Lord. That's how we wait silently and with a sense of confidence. When we wait for God to direct our steps, He does! When we trust Him to meet our needs, He will!

The mind of man plans his way, but the LORD directs his steps.

PROVERBS 16:9

BIBLE READING: PSALM 48:9–14

CHARLES SWINDOLL

NOVEMBER

-18-

Rejoicing is clearly a spiritual command. To ignore it, I need to remind you, is disobedience. In place of worry, start spending time enjoying the release of your humor. Find the bright side, the sunny side of life. Deliberately look for things that are funny during your day. Loosen up and laugh freely. Laugh more often. Consciously stay aware of the importance of a cheerful countenance. Live lightheartedly!

I have set the LORD continually
before me . . . therefore my heart is glad.

PSALM 16:8—9

BIBLE READING: PSALM 16

NOVEMBER

-19-

What makes worry such an enemy of joy? WORRY FORCES US TO FOCUS ON THE WRONG THINGS!

Instead of essentials, we worry about nonessentials. Rather than looking at the known blessings that God provides us today—so abundantly, so consistently—we worry about the unknown and uncertain events of tomorrow. Invariably, when we focus on the wrong things, we miss the main thing that life is all about.

Do not be worried about your life.

MATTHEW 6:25

BIBLE READING: PSALM 146

NOVEMBER
-20-

A spirit of gratitude makes the weeks before Christmas a celebration rather than a marathon. Four weeks before Christmas, let's be thankful for the spring of the year. During the third week, be thankful for summer, in the second week, for autumn, and the final week, for winter. Instead of fretting about how many shopping days are left, reflect on wonderful memories of each season of the year. As you do, I think you'll find that the crowds aren't nearly so irritating and the music in the malls may even be downright enjoyable.

See the works of God, Who is awesome in His deeds.

PSALM 66:5

BIBLE READING: PSALM 66:5–7; 1 THESSALONIANS 5:16–18

NOVEMBER

-21-

The determined, decreed dimension of God's will has four qualities: (1) It is absolute. (2) It is immutable (unchangeable). (3) It is unconditional. (4) It is always in complete harmony with His plan and His nature. In other words, the decreed will of God will be holy, it will be just, it will be good, it will be righteous; therefore it will be best.

God causes all things to work
together for good to those who love God.

ROMANS 8:28

BIBLE READING: ROMANS 8:28–39

CHARLES SWINDOLL

NOVEMBER

-22-

Humility is not how you dress, it in not the money you make, it is not where you live, it's not what you drive, it is not even how you look. We're never once commanded by God to "look" humble. Humility is an attitude. It is an attitude of the heart. An attitude of the mind. It is knowing your proper place. Never talking down or looking down because someone may be of a financial level less than yours. It is knowing your role and fulfilling it for God's glory and praise.

Have this attitude in yourselves which was also in Christ Jesus.

PHILIPPIANS 2:5

BIBLE READING: PHILIPPIANS 2:1—11

NOVEMBER

-23-

"No purpose of Yours can be thwarted." Remember that conclusion. Don't scissor that out of your Bible. Mark it and memorize it. When God says it will be done, it will be done. If it makes me unhappy? It makes me unhappy. If it hurts? It hurts. If it ruins my reputation? It ruins my reputation. God says it shall be done and His purpose will not be thwarted . . . or He is not sovereign.

"I know that You can do all things,
and that no purpose of Yours can be thwarted."

JOB 42:2

BIBLE READING: PROVERBS 28:26; 1 CORINTHIANS 1:25; 8:3

CHARLES SWINDOLL

NOVEMBER

-24-

When we are Spirit-filled and therefore rightly related to the Spirit of God:

- We have an inner dynamic to handle life's pressures.
- We are able to by joyful . . . regardless.
- We have the capacity to grasp the deep things of God that He discloses to us in His Word.
- We are able to love and be loved in return.

Be filled with the Spirit.

EPHESIANS 5:18

BIBLE READING: EPHESIANS 5:11–21

NOVEMBER
-25-

Let me ask you a straight-out question: Do you, personally, pray? Now notice that I didn't say, "Do you listen when the preacher prays or when your parents pray?" I didn't say, "Do you know a good Bible study on prayer?" I asked: "Do *you*, personally pray?"

Howard Taylor once wrote of his father's discipline in prayer: "The sun never rose on China for forty years but that God did not find my father [Hudson Taylor] in prayer."

I love the LORD, because He hears
my voice and my supplications.

PSALM 116:1

BIBLE READING: PSALM 116:1—11

CHARLES SWINDOLL

NOVEMBER
-26-

The connecting link between a holy God and a sinful person is God's love, which activates His grace, which, in turn, sets in motion His mercy. They're like divine dominoes that bump up against one another. He loves us not because of something in ourselves but because of something in Himself.

God, being rich in mercy, . . . loved us,
even when we were dead in our transgressions.

EPHESIANS 2:4–5

BIBLE READING: 1 JOHN 2:6, 15; 3:18; 4:21

NOVEMBER

-27-

Just the word "Thanskgiving" prompts the spirit of humility—genuine gratitude to God for His mercy, His abundance, His protection, His smile of favor. At this holiday, as at no other, we count our blessings. And we run out of time before we come back to the soil and the sun and the rain that combine their efforts to produce the miracle of life, resulting in food for our stomachs and shelter for our bodies . . . direct gifts from our God of grace.

Come and see the works of God, Who is awesome in His deeds.

PSALM 66:5

BIBLE READING: PSALM 66

NOVEMBER

-28-

Self-denial doesn't come naturally. It's a learned virtue, encouraged by few and modeled by even fewer, especially among those we describe as Type A personalities. Prophets are notorious for exhibiting this temperament, which makes Elijah all the more remarkable. Without hedging in heroism, he was as soft as clay in his Master's hands. His was a life of power, because he had come to the place where he welcomed the death of his own desires, if it meant the display of God's greater glory.

He who dwells in the shelter of the
Most High will abide in the shadow of the Almighty.

PSALM 91:1

BIBLE READING: PSALM 91:1–10; 1 KINGS 18:36–46

NOVEMBER

-29-

You know what? God personally cares about the things that worry us. He cares more about them than we care about them: those things that hang in our minds as nagging, aching, worrisome thoughts. . . . He cares. You are His personal concern.

Casting all your anxiety on Him, because He cares for you.

1 PETER 5:7

BIBLE READING: PSALM 18:1–6, 46–50

CHARLES SWINDOLL

NOVEMBER

-30-

The Spirit-filled saint is a song-filled saint! Your melody is broadcast right into heaven. Never mind how beautiful or pitiful you may sound. You are not auditioning for the choir; you're making melody with your heart.

SING OUT!

If you listen closely, you may hear the hosts of heaven shouting for joy. Then again, it might be your neighbor . . . screaming for relief.

Sing praises to His name, for it is lovely.

PSALM 135:3

BIBLE READING: PSALM 135:1–7

DECEMBER

HE CAME TO SHOW US THE WAY.

DECEMBER

-1-

It's not too early to give some things away this Christmas. Not just on Christmas Day, but during all the days leading up to December 25. We could call these daily gifts "our Christmas projects." Maybe one per day from now 'til then. Here are a few suggestions.

- Mend a quarrel.
- Seek out a forgotten friend.
- Write a long overdue love note.
- Gladden the heart of a child.

This is Christianity, isn't it?

God is love, and the one who abides in love abides in God.

1 JOHN 4:16

BIBLE READING: 1 JOHN 4:7–21

CHARLES SWINDOLL

DECEMBER

-2-

Ordinary days can become extraordinary. They can become so pivotal they change the entire course of life.

How about the day Jesus arrived? There wasn't one citizen in Judea who awoke that morning expecting the day to bring such a life-changing event in the village of Bethlehem. Yet before that day had ended, Mary's little Lamb was born . . . and the world would never be the same.

Today in the city of David there has been born for you a Savior, who is Christ the Lord.

LUKE 2:11

BIBLE READING: LUKE 2:1–20; ISAIAH 53:1–6

DECEMBER

-3-

COURAGE. David had it when he grabbed his sling. Daniel demonstrated it when he refused to worship Nebuchadnezzar's statue. Elijah evidenced it when he faced the prophets of Baal. Job showed it when he was covered with boils and surrounded by misunderstandings. Moses used it when he stood against Pharaoh and refused to be intimidated. The fact is, *it's impossible to live victoriously for Christ without courage.*

Be strong and courageous!

JOSHUA 1:6, 7, 9

BIBLE READING: HEBREWS 13:6; PROVERBS 29:25

DECEMBER

-4-

B e who you are. Give yourself the O.K. to break the mold and exercise your God-given freedom.

God, in grace, has purchased you from bondage. Christ has literally set you free. The Spirit of the Lord has provided long-awaited liberty. Give yourself permission to lift your wings and feel the exhilaration of a soaring life-style.

Where the Spirit of the Lord is, there is liberty.

2 CORINTHIANS 3:17

BIBLE READING: GALATIANS 1:6—10

DECEMBER

-5-

As the year draws to a close, Christmas offers its wonderful message. Emmanuel. God with us. He who resided in Heaven, co-equal and co-eternal with the Father and the Spirit, willingly descended into our world. He breathed our air, felt our pain, knew our sorrows, and died for our sins. He didn't come to frighten us, but to show us the way to warmth and safety.

He will be great and will be called the Son of the Most High.

LUKE 1:32

BIBLE READING: LUKE 1:46–55

DECEMBER
-6-

Jesus Christ carried out the most innovative, creative plan this world will ever know. From the virgin birth to the death and the resurrection to the soon-coming of Christ, the plan of Almighty God is rich with innovation and creativity. It had never been done before. It will never be done again. It was a once and for all Master Plan only the Creator could envision.

The one who does the will of God lives forever.

1 JOHN 2:17

BIBLE READING: 1 John 2:15—29

DECEMBER

-7-

How is winsomeness cultivated—and communicated in our homes and among our other contacts? I suggest three specific projects

1. Start each day with pleasant words.
2. Smile more often.
3. Express appreciation and encouragement.

Ask God to be winsome through you.

A man's counsel is sweet to his friend.

PROVERBS 27:9

BIBLE READING: PROVERBS 17:22; PSALM 126:1–6

CHARLES SWINDOLL

DECEMBER

-8-

For Christmas one year we bought our children what was called "Ant City." This consisted of clear plastic plates on either side, filled with sand and ants. We watched as they tunneled their way around, leaving a maze of trails.

In a similar fashion, God scrutinizes our paths. From where we are, all we see is what's immediately around us. But from God's vantage point, He sees exactly where we've been and precisely where we're going.

The path of the righteous . . .
shines brighter and brighter until the full day.

PROVERBS 4:18

BIBLE READING: PSALM 16:11; 27:11; 23:3; 25:4

DECEMBER

- 9 -

We all need roots *and* wings. But most of us are long on the former and short on the latter.

Whether it's a longed-for trip to Europe or a relaxing weekend at a picturesque Bed and Breakfast, a fishing trip to Alaska or an afternoon canoe trip down a nearby river, try some winged adventure. Expand your world, free your mind, and calm your nerves. Don't wait!

A wise heart knows the proper time and procedure.

ECCLESIASTES 8:5

BIBLE READING: MARK 6

CHARLES SWINDOLL

DECEMBER

-10-

God does not dispense strength and encouragement like a druggist fills a prescription. The Lord doesn't promise to give us something to *take* so we can handle our weary moments. He promises us *Himself.* That is all. And that is enough.

He himself is our peace.

EPHESIANS 2:14, NIV

BIBLE READING: PSALM 6:6–7; ISAIAH 40:28–31

DECEMBER

-11-

Christians are not supernaturally protected from the aches or the pains of living on this globe. Christians can be unfairly treated. We can suffer financial reversals, we can be taken advantage of, abused, neglected, and divorced by uncaring mates. Then how can we expect to be joyful, unlike those around us? Because God promises that deep within He will give us peace . . . an unexplainable, illogical inner peace.

In Me you may have peace. In the world you have tribulation, but take courage; I have overcome the world.

JOHN 16:33

BIBLE READING: JOHN 16:23–33

CHARLES SWINDOLL

DECEMBER

-12-

I sometimes think of the Holy Spirit as a deep-sea diver who goes searching for treasure. The diver drops off the side of the boat . . . probing through all the mysteries of the deep that the human eye cannot see from above. Finally he surfaces again, bringing treasures from some sunken vessel.

The Spirit of God, in the same manner, searches the deepest realms of the wisdom of God to lift out truths we need to understand and brings them to our attention. What magnificent work!

The Spirit searches all things, even the depths of God.

1 CORINTHIANS 2:10

BIBLE READING: JOHN 14:16—24

DECEMBER

-13-

Circumstances occur that could easily crush us. They may originate on the job or at home or even during the weekend when we are relaxing. Unexpectedly, they come. Immediately we have a choice to make. . . . We can hand the circumstances to God and ask Him to take control or we can roll up our mental sleeves and slug it out. Joy awaits our decision.

My God will supply all your needs
according to His riches in glory in Christ Jesus.

PHILIPPIANS 4:19

BIBLE READING: 1 CHRONICLES 29:11; PSALM 107:1–9

CHARLES SWINDOLL

DECEMBER

-14-

I have often thought of Jesus' words when He was only hours removed from the cross. In His prayer to the Father, He said, "I glorified You on the earth, having accomplished the work which You have given Me to do" (John 17:4). A little over thirty-three years after His arrival in Bethlehem, there He stood in Jerusalem, saying, in effect, "It's a wrap." He had done everything the Father sent Him to do . . . and in the final analysis, that's what mattered.

"I glorified You on the earth,
having accomplished the work which You have given Me to do."

JOHN 17:4

BIBLE READING: JOHN 17:1—26

DECEMBER

-15-

Do you long for God? I've got great news! In an even greater way—greater than you could ever imagine—He longs to be gracious to you. He is offering you all the things you hunger for. The table is loaded, and He is smiling, waiting for you to sit down and enjoy the feast He prepared with you in mind. Have a seat—grace is being served.

The LORD longs to be gracious to you,
and therefore He waits on high to have compassion on you.

ISAIAH 30:18

BIBLE READING: ROMANS 5

DECEMBER

-16-

When God is in our heart of compassion, prompting us to get involved in helping others . . . when He is in our acts of generosity, honoring our support of those engaged in ministry . . . and when He is in our strong commitment, using our sacrifices to bless other lives, He does not forget us in our need. It is all so beautiful, so simple, so right.

From everyone who has been
given much, much will be required.

LUKE 12:48

BIBLE READING: LUKE 12:35–48

DECEMBER

-17-

A sculptor was asked how he could carve a lion's head out of a large block of marble. "I just chip away everything that doesn't look like a lion's head," was his reply. God works away in our being and chips away everything that doesn't look like Christ—the impatience, the short temper, the pride. He's shaping us into His image. That's His predetermined plan. And He's committed to it. Nothing we can do will dissuade Him from that plan. He is relentless.

If we are faithless, he remains faithful;
for He cannot deny Himself.

2 TIMOTHY 2:13

BIBLE READING: 2 TIMOTHY 2:8—13

CHARLES SWINDOLL

DECEMBER

-18-

While Rome was busy making history, God arrived. He pitched His fleshly tent in silence on the straw . . . in a stable . . . under a star. The world didn't even notice. Reeling from the wake of Alexander the Great . . . Herod the Great . . . Augustus the Great, the world overlooked Mary's little Lamb.

It still does.

Behold the virgin shall be with child and shall bear a Son, and they shall call His name Immanuel.

MATTHEW 1:23

BIBLE READING: MATTHEW 1:18–25; 2:1–23

DECEMBER

-19-

Part of my training in the Marine Corps included some tips for surviving in combat. One was: Always dig a hole big enough for two, preferably three. Inevitable, the strain of battle will cause you to go weak in the knees. You need somebody near you, to help you stay strong.

God has designed His family to be that sort of support network. Nobody can handle all the pressure over the long haul. Companionship and accountability are essential!

Bear one another's burdens,
and thereby fulfill the law of Christ.

GALATIANS 6:2

BIBLE READING: GALATIANS 6

CHARLES SWINDOLL

DECEMBER
-20-

Even in the midst of Job's pain and struggle with God's mysterious plan, there comes a magnificent presence of divine mercy—*chesed*.

When we're suffering unfair treatment, there is mercy with God. When we're enduring grief, there is mercy. All these earthly struggles are no accident. God is in the midst of them, working out His sovereign will. Yes, it's a mystery, which means we need His mercy to endure.

You have granted me life and lovingkindness [chesed]; and Your care has preserved my spirit.

JOB 10:12

BIBLE READING: PSALM 17:6–12

DECEMBER

-21-

A commentator once suggested that since Psalm twenty-three is written from the viewpoint of a shepherd and his sheep, that last verse could represent God's sheep dogs named Goodness and Mercy.

Sheep of God, do you realize that these two faithful "dogs" watch over you and care for you? Their presence reminds us that relief has come. They nuzzle us back into the shadow of the Shepherd, who graciously welcomes us and forgives us.

Surely goodness and mercy
shall follow me all the days of my life.

PSALM 23:6, NKJV

BIBLE READING: ISAIAH 40:9–11

CHARLES SWINDOLL

DECEMBER

-22-

Since God has "an appointed time for everything," an ideal method of time management is T-R-U-S-T, putting the pressure back into His hands:

- Time dragging? TRUST.
- Deadlines arriving? TRUST.
- Habits lingering? TRUST.
- Diet getting old? TRUST.
- Unwanted guests staying? TRUST.
- Prayers not being answered? TRUST.

There is an appointed time for everything.

ECCLESIASTES 3:1

BIBLE READING: PSALM 40:1–4; 130:5–6

DECEMBER

-23-

The Lord's faithfulness never diminishes.

Even when you blow it? Yes, even when you blow it. Even when you make several stupid decisions? Even when you make several stupid decisions. Even when your marriage fails? Even when your marriage fails. Even when you knew better? Even when you knew better. His faithfulness never diminishes.

His compassions never fail. They are
new every morning; great is Your faithfulness.

LAMENTATIONS 3:22–23

BIBLE READING: LAMENTATIONS 3:19–38

CHARLES SWINDOLL

DECEMBER
-24-

Spend a full day in quietness. Sundays are great days to do that. Set aside at least part of the afternoon to be completely quiet. Meditation is a lost art in this modern, hurry-up world. I suggest you revive it. Not by endlessly repeating some mantra to get into some other frame of mind. Not that. Simply and silently wait before God. Read a passage of Scripture and let it speak. Say nothing. Just sit silently.

The LORD is good to those who
wait for Him, to the person who seeks Him.

LAMENTATIONS 3:25

BIBLE READING: PSALM 147:7–11

DECEMBER
-25-

When Isaiah predicted that a child would be born . . . everybody should have listened, but they didn't.

Eight hundred years later (!) in a feeding trough in lowly Bethlehem . . . the cry from that Infant's throat broke the centuries of silence. For the first time in time, God's voice could actually be heard coming from vocal cords. Everybody should have believed, but they didn't.

A child will be born to us, and . . .
His name will be called . . . Prince of Peace.

ISAIAH 9:6

BIBLE READING: ISAIAH 44:24–45; LUKE 1:26–38

CHARLES SWINDOLL

DECEMBER

-26-

Light is a symbol of purity. God is absolutely resplendent purity. He is flawless in His holiness. "In Him is no darkness at all." Imagine, not one dark thought, not one dark motive. In His nature and in His will there is no darkness at all.

When we lay our sins before Him, He cleanses us. As His children, He gives us a purity that matches His own, and thus we can fellowship with Him. Imagine that.

God is light, and in Him there is no darkness at all.

1 JOHN 1:5

BIBLE READING: PROVERBS 13:9; JOHN 3

DECEMBER

-27-

God is sovereign over all the events of our lives. Not one detail escapes His attention. The very hairs of our head are numbered. He knows everything about us. Furthermore, He is immutably faithful. And yet He deliberately surprises us with difficult assignments, premature or unexpected deaths, lost jobs, and disappointing circumstances along the journey. Let's face it, it's a mystery.

The very hairs of your head are all numbered.

MATTHEW 10:30

BIBLE READING: JOB 28:24; PSALM 139:3

DECEMBER

-28-

Wherever you are in this journey called life, wherever you may be employed, wherever you may be in your domestic situation, wherever you may be in your age, your health, or your lifestyle, God may be preparing you for a great surprise in order to find you faithful. Rather than running from Him, let me suggest the opposite: Run *toward* Him.

He who does not take his cross
and follow after Me is not worthy of Me.

MATTHEW 10:38

BIBLE READING: MATTHEW 10:24–39

DECEMBER

-29-

Are you weary? Heavy laden? Distressed? Come to the Savior. Come immediately, come repeatedly, come boldly. And be at rest. When was the last time you came to the Lord, all alone, and gave Him your load of care?

No wonder you're weary!

> LORD, You have heard the desire
> of the humble; . . . You will cause Your ear to hear.
>
> PSALM 10:17, NKJV

BIBLE READING: MARK 11:24; PSALM 31:14

CHARLES SWINDOLL

DECEMBER

-30-

The godly life is never easy. Rewarding? Yes. Worthwhile? A thousand times yes. But it's never easy.

Truth is, if you really want to break the boredom syndrome, commit yourself to Jesus Christ. Life will start comin' at you!

Many are the afflictions of the
righteous, but the LORD delivers him out of them all.

PSALM 34:19

BIBLE READING: PSALM 34:15–22

DECEMBER

-31-

We can only see the present and the past. The future is a little frightening to us. So we need to hold onto God's hand and trust Him to calm our fears. And at those times when we're stubborn and resisting and God shakes us by the shoulders to get our attention, we're reminded that we don't call our own shots, that God has a plan for us, mysterious though it may seem, and we want to be in the center of it.

The LORD has set apart the godly man
for Himself; the LORD hears when I call to Him.

PSALM 4:3

BIBLE READING: PSALM 118:8; 40:4

CHARLES SWINDOLL

ACKNOWLEDGMENTS

Grateful acknowledgment is made to the following publishers for permission to reprint this copyrighted material. All copyrights are held by the author, Charles R. Swindoll.

Growing Strong in the Seasons of Life, (Sisters, Oregon: Multnomah, 1983)

Flying Closer to the Flame, (Nashville: W Publishing, 1993).

The Finishing Touch, (Nashville: W Publishing, 1994).

Laugh Again, (Nashville: W Publishing, 1994).

Hope Again, (Nashville: W Publishing, 1996).

David: A Man of Passion and Destiny, (Nashville: W Publishing, 1997).

Joseph: A Man of Integrity and Forgiveness, (Nashville: W Publishing, 1998).

Esther: A Woman of Strength and Dignity, (Nashville: W Publishing, 1999).

The Mystery of God's Will, (Nashville: W Publishing, 1999).

Moses: A Man of Selfless Dedication, (Nashville: W Publishing, 1999).

Perfect Trust, (Nashville: J. Countryman, 2000).

Elijah: A Man of Heroism and Humility, (Nashville: W Publishing, 2000).

Day by Day with Charles Swindoll, (Nashville: W Publishing, 2000).

The Darkness and the Dawn, (Nashville: W Publishing, 2001)

Paul: A Man of Grace and Grit, (Nashville: W Publishing, 2002)